DATE DUE

MULTINATIONAL CRIME

STUDIES IN CRIME, LAW, AND JUSTICE

Series Editor: James A. Inciardi,
Division of Criminal Justice, University of Delaware

Studies in Crime, Law and Justice contains original research formulations and new analytic perspectives on continuing important issues of crime and the criminal justice and legal systems. Volumes are research based but are written in nontechnical language to allow for use in courses in criminal justice, criminology, law, social problems, and related subjects.

MULTINATIONAL CRIME
Terrorism, Espionage, Drug & Arms Trafficking

BY

John M. Martin
Anne T. Romano

STUDIES IN CRIME, LAW, AND JUSTICE ■ Volume 9

SAGE Publications
International Educational and Professional Publisher
Newbury Park   London   New Delhi

For information address:

SAGE Publications, Inc.
2455 Teller Road
Newbury Park, California 91320

SAGE Publications Ltd.
6 Bonhill Street
London EC2A 4PU
United Kingdom

SAGE Publications India Pvt. Ltd.
M-32 Market
Greater Kailash I
New Delhi 110 048 India

Printed in the United States of America

Library of Congress Cataloging-in-Publication Data

Martin, John McCullough.
  Multinational crime : terrorism, espionage, drug & arms
trafficking / John M. Martin, Anne T. Romano.
      p.   cm.   — (Studies in crime, law, and justice ; v. 9)
  Includes bibliographical references and index.
  ISBN 0-8039-4597-3.   — ISBN 0-8039-4598-1 (pbk.)
  1. Transnational crime.   2. Terrorism.   3. Drug traffic.
I. Romano, Anne T.   II. Title.   III. Series.
HV6252.M37   1992
364.1'35—dc20   91-44786
                                                             CIP

92   93   94   95   96   10   9   8   7   6   5   4   3   2   1

Sage Production Editor: Judith L. Hunter

Contents

Acknowledgments

For permission to reprint copyrighted material, the authors and publisher gratefully acknowledge the following:

Burns, J. F. (1990, February 4). Afghans: Now they blame America. *The New York Times Magazine.* Copyright ©1990 by The New York Times Company. Reprinted by permission.

Ibrahim, Y. M. (1990, January 30). Trial of accused mastermind in bombings begins in Paris. *New York Times,* p. A2. Copyright ©1990 by The New York Times Company. Reprinted by permission.

Lee, R.W. III (1989). *The white labyrinth: Cocaine and political power.* New Brunswick, NJ: Transaction Publishers. Copyright ©1989 by Transaction Publishers. Reprinted by permission.

Massing, M. (1990, March 4). In the cocaine war. . .the jungle is winning. *The New York Times Magazine.* Copyright ©1990 by The New York Times Company. Reprinted by permission.

Penn, S. (1990, March 22). Asian connection: Chinese gangsters fill a narcotics gap left by U.S. drive on Mafia. *Wall Street Journal,* p. 1. Reprinted by permission of *Wall Street Journal,* ©1990 by Dow Jones & Company, Inc. All Rights Reserved Worldwide.

Reuters (1990, January 15). Moscow reports the capture of a longtime American spy. *New York Times,* p. 1. Reprinted with permission of Reuters.

Waint, J. A. (1985). Narcotics in the golden triangle. *The Washington Quarterly, 8*(4), 125-140. Reprinted by permission of The MIT Press, Cambridge, Massachusetts, and the Center for Strategic and International Studies, Georgetown University. Copyright © by the Center for Strategic and International Studies, Georgetown University, and the Massachusetts Institute of Technology.

Foreword

Every once in a while a book comes along that leads the readers to realize that they have come into contact either with a new perspective on reality or with an old perspective presented in a strikingly new way. I think of Thomas Kuhn's *Structure of Scientific Revolutions,* or, in the social problems area, of Michael Harrington's *The Other America.* This book of John Martin and Anne Romano's is a book of that type. The book does not reveal what we did not know. There are abundant reports about terrorism, espionage, drug and arms trafficking; the book quotes from many of them. Martin and Romano have taken this information and have cast it into a perspective in which these criminal activities are seen to have a meaning quite different from the one that permeates our ordinary or scholarly discussions about them. When news breaks about these activities in the press or on TV, we are inclined to think of the individual who drove the truck into the Marine barracks in Lebanon, or the spy who suddenly gets caught, or the drug dealer busted in a police raid. Martin and Romano are telling us that, generally, these are not individual acts. They are part of a highly complicated, well-organized system that functions very much like a modern international business corporation. Drug trafficking, for example, is not the behavior of a daring, secretive, and clever operator; it is a complex international business system, deeply touching the lives of peasant farmers, political leaders in the nation's capitol, or the highly competent business men and women who make the system go, and reap enormous profits from it. Therefore, in order for us to understand them, to perceive their broader meaning, they must be studied as systematic behavior, in the full context of their economic, political, and cultural aspects.

The book is not the presentation of a theory. Rather, it describes a method of study that may result in a theory. As the authors insist, there is no theory of these criminal activities. Policies and programs seeking to prevent them are frequently hit-and-miss affairs, responding to popular demands to "do something about it," or pragmatic reactions to a crisis. If these international activities are to be prevented, we must know clearly what we are trying to prevent. Herein lies the value of this book. It describes the international and organizational character of these activities and puts them into a perspective in which we understand better what we are trying to explain. For this we are indebted to John Martin and Anne Romano. A new field of criminology is in the making.

In one sense it is understandable why criminologists have not paid more attention to these international forms of crime. Realistic and reliable data are hard to come by; it is not very easy to search out the meaning they have for the various parties involved; and it will require enormous effort to study these activities in all their economic, political, and cultural aspects. As the authors describe it, this requires an interdisciplinary method that may not be attractive to specialized scholars.

Finally, it is a field in which values and interests are very much at stake. These do not lend themselves easily to empirical research. The authors wisely point out that, even if the best of theories should be developed, decisions about the prevention of these international crimes are generally made in light of the values and interests, particularly the national security interests, of the parties involved.

We can only hope that criminologists and other scholars of the international economic and political scene will continue where this book leaves off, and, guided by the perspectives that Martin and Romano have so clearly given us, arrive at a better understanding of these crimes, which may result in more effective remedies.

Joseph P. Fitzpatrick, SJ
Professor Emeritus of Sociology
Fordham University

Preface

In the course of writing this book it became clear to us that there were few, if any, good organizational models available in the literature of criminology and criminal justice to guide us in the study of what we call *multinational systemic crime.* We therefore proceeded inductively, from various descriptive sources, to construct most of the different concepts and interrelationships described in the following chapters.

These analytical tasks drew upon both the theory and the methods of sociology, and also upon some understanding and use of political science, history, economics, and anthropology. Our experience in writing this book convinces us that any fruitful study of global criminal organizations, such as those we examine in the pages ahead, requires a multidisciplinary approach. If this conclusion is borne out through the experience of others, then significant changes may be desirable in undergraduate and graduate education in both criminology and criminal justice. This may become particularly apparent as these two fields develop an increasing interest in understanding global crime and its control.

Those interested in studying multinational crime might also be encouraged to view skeptically statements by governments and their spokesmen on this subject, since their frequently covert complicity in such crime has long been marked by disinformation, deception, and outright cover-ups. Hence, before being accepted, statements and reports from such politically sensitive sources about terrorism, arms-trafficking, and other multinational crimes would appear to merit special scrutiny.

Unlike the control of most domestic crime, the control of multinational crime appears frequently to involve problems of jurisdiction, sovereignty, and common purpose not always easily resolved in the relations between nations. The absence of shared and consistently applied legal principles, the lack of restraint of national self-interests, and the nonexistence of a widely supported international criminal justice authority for the purpose of enforcement also contribute to an inability to effectively control multinational crime. Moreover, and perhaps most important, much of such crime arises from political, economic, religious, and other historical and structural roots, which do not appear to be addressed effectively by even an international exercise of police power. In fact, the use of force often appears not to eliminate but to escalate "terrorism" arising out of age-old struggles for territorial integrity and political self-determination. Also, the leaders of the vast intelligence communities of modern nation-states seldom appear to reduce the work of their global webs of espionage because of the threat of the arrest and punishment of agents by foreign powers. Further, the use of police power over the decades does not seem to have seriously interrupted the wide-ranging commerce in illegal drugs and firearms between source and consumer nations. Wherever the best response to such multinational crime may rest, based on experience, it is difficult to accept that it rests with the use of force. In international affairs, force may solve many problems; it may also create many others. History does not convincingly suggest that force is a viable policy to rely on for containing multinational crime.

Nevertheless, force continues to be a seductive and popular central policy for the leaders of victim nations to endorse. Why? Perhaps this holds true because such policy lends substantial commitment to the expansion of police and military bureaucracies, which represent powerful constituencies in almost every nation-state. Moreover, in conservative contexts the articulation of such a policy by government always seems to stimulate a widespread endorsement of national leaders by common citizens who demand "tough-minded" measures. Generally it is only after the passage of years that it becomes clear to serious observers that such policies of force have evidenced serious deficiencies in the containment of "terrorism," drug-trafficking, and other forms of multinational crime. Indeed, in some ways force may even have been counterproductive. But as the years have passed, the national leaders who initiated such policies and sustained them have themselves usually been replaced by a later generation of elites, who, in turn, face many of the same continuing multinational threats. In such circumstances the policy cycle of force may then be repeated by the new leaders, with sometimes little change occurring, or even contemplated, with respect to altering the structural roots of multinational criminal systems.

In reviewing history it is difficult to tell whether newly elected, or otherwise recently installed, national leaders have been ignorant of the lessons of the past regarding the limits of force when applied to multinational crime, or whether they have shrewdly professed ignorance for tactical reasons. Perhaps they have simply acted out of firm and honest ideological conviction. But in the end the result appears to be the same: Force often continues to be applied as a keystone of government policy and this, in turn, is applauded by a broad constituency, while multinational criminal organizations continue to expand their global networks and consolidate their power in the context of an increasingly "borderless" world.

As this book is being edited, a new multinational crime scandal has burst onto the world scene—the crime-ridden world bank, the Bank of Credit and Commerce International (BCCI). The investigations of this multinational criminal organization have, at this point, scarcely begun, but already at least two things seem clear. First, this criminal corporation practiced large-scale fraud in scores of countries, while at the same time meeting the clandestine banking needs of other global criminal organizations engaged in terrorism, espionage, drug- and arms-trafficking. In hindsight it seems inevitable that such criminal macro-systems would require the logistical support of an equally criminal world bank. The second thing that seems evident at present—but whose full meaning remains unclear—is that BCCI was created, funded, and operated by Muslim entrepreneurs of the Third World, many of whom had, and continue to have, close relations with Western leaders and governments.

Given the widespread existence and interrelations of various global criminal organizations, it is perhaps reasonable at this juncture to suspect that there has been an extensive, powerful, criminal, shadow global web that sometimes fulfilled the clandestine and often illegal needs of governments, and sometimes simply traded for profit. The leaders and supporters of such multinational criminal organizations, both inside and outside government, may perhaps be properly called the global outlaws and brigands of modern times. That they often operate beyond the effective legal reach of their victim nation-states is possibly a sign of their great skill and resourcefulness.

* * *

We wish to acknowledge the assistance provided by our students at Fordham College and Nassau Community College in terms of their comments and criticisms of many of the ideas expressed in this book. Their reactions were significantly useful in our formulation and reformulation of key aspects of the book's eventual presentations. We also wish to express appreciation for their interest and assistance to Frank P. Williams III, Richard H. Ward, Mark H. Moore, Gerald M. Shattuck, James F. Haran, and Ronald Heffernan.

Most particularly, the detailed comments about and the editing of an earlier draft of the final manuscript by Joseph P. Fitzpatrick and Thelma Martin are most deeply valued.

Last, we thank the staffs at the Darien (Connecticut) Library and Duane Library at Fordham University for their courtesy and cooperation.

John M. Martin
Anne T. Romano
Siasconset, Massachusetts
August 1991

Introduction

For more than 150 years criminology and, more recently, the newer field of criminal justice have been producing a rich and varied literature about crime. From the start, robbery, homicide, theft, assault, arson, and other traditional or conventional crimes were given serious study. Various, often conflicting, theories were developed to explain such crimes. Different policies and programs were also offered to control conventional crimes. More recently substantial attention has been paid to concepts such as professional, organized, and white-collar crime. Since the 1970s the concept of political crime has also been given a place in criminology and criminal justice. Together with conventional crimes, these more recently added concepts may be used to identify the major forms of domestic crime in the United States and other modern societies.

This book is not about domestic crime. Instead it is about what the authors call *multinational systemic crime*—that is, crimes by various kinds of organizations that operate across national boundaries and in two or more countries simultaneously. This concept is a collective term referring to a variety of criminal behavior systems, of which four will be considered in the chapters ahead: terrorism, espionage, drug-trafficking, and arms-trafficking. Each carries a strong connotation of evil. Each is commonly defined as a serious threat by national governments when directed against their interests. Sometimes one or more of the four may be called a threat to a country's "national security." On the other hand, nation-states have sometimes called the same or very similar behaviors by more positive names when they carry them out against others. For example, the saturation bombing of civilian populations in German and Japanese cities during World War II, although it certainly terrorized the civilians targeted, was said to "dehouse" the enemy and was defined as "area bombing"—not terrorism—by the Allies (Fussell, 1989, p. 16). Or to take another example, extensive smuggling of opium into China by British and American traders during the early part of the nineteenth century, in persistent violation of Chinese law, was defined as essential trade—not drug-trafficking—by Britain and the United States (Beeching, 1975).

It should be clear at the outset that such crime is not new. Much of it has been occurring for generations, some for centuries. Today, as in the past, multinational systemic crime usually appears to be well organized and integrated with powerful legal and illegal institutions of various nation-states. For example: One government may legally ship arms to client rebel armies, whose forces have illegally invaded the territory and are attacking the civilians and the government of another nation; organized crime groups within a nation may trade in contraband—for example, illegal drugs—using transportation and banking systems in various source and transit countries; or citizens from one nation may be recruited and trained by their government's intelligence agencies to establish spy rings overseas in order to steal national security secrets from the government of another nation. Such networks as these, which transcend national boundaries, would appear to fall well outside of what are generally perceived to be the accepted concepts that describe domestic crime. Even the concept of organized crime substantially fails to describe adequately such diverse multinational criminal networks, although some of them organized for economic gain may be rooted in or have emerged from more traditional domestic organized crime groups. For example, during the past several decades, some traditional local criminal groups have become very wealthy and powerful global criminal organizations on the basis of the vast profits derived from drug-trafficking. In the case of the island-based Sicilian Mafia, Claire Sterling (1990) describes how local bosses became multinational titans on the basis of the profits made in the heroin trade, all since the 1950s.

To a major degree and in a variety of complex ways, as we will see in the chapters that follow, multinational crime systems are often interrelated in the reality of today's world. And different parts of this world are themselves rapidly becoming more accessible and interdependent because of, among other things, the dissolution of traditional political and trade barriers, acceleration of migration and immigration, worldwide airlifting of cargo and passengers, and instantaneous worldwide communication.

But more than the speed and ease of transportation and communication are involved in the notion that the world is rapidly becoming more interdependent. Not interdependent in the sense of the dominance of a single nation-state, or integrated in any cultural sense, for certainly intranational and international conflicts continue. Rather the world is more interdependent in the sense that the various nation-states, large and small, rich and poor, are becoming increasingly dependent upon one another for their economic, social, and political well-being. Thus, for example, what happens in Peru with regard to the coca crop has an impact on the national cocaine crisis in the United States. Or again, what happened in Iran in 1979 with regard to hostage-taking after the fall of the Shah had a most dramatic impact on American politics and the career of President Jimmy Carter and later, in the 1980s because of the Iran-Contra Affair, on the reputation of President Ronald Reagan. Additionally, the loss of Vietnam raises the stakes the United States has in its other military bases in the Pacific. Finally, when international trade policy lowers the price paid for Colombian coffee, one of that country's leading legal exports, this, in turn, increases the economic importance of cocaine, its leading illegal export. The list goes on, but the principle of growing interdependence seems clear.

It is within this context that multinational crime systems exist, and apparently are becoming more interrelated, and, it would seem, are also becoming frequently more expansive, powerful, and difficult to precisely identify, describe, and control. In strict law-enforcement terms, such systems also appear to present many perplexing and unresolved jurisdictional issues. Not the least of these are problems of extradition from one country to another, and the authority of police agents from one nation to operate within the territory of another. Such authority raises special difficulties when the targets of investigation are powerful and influential citizens of the host nation. The difficulties are compounded if the investigation is directed against ranking officials of the government of the host nation.

The general idea that in recent decades the world has increasingly become a global village, and that crime itself has become globalized, is becoming recognized in the criminological literature (see, for example, Adler, Mueller & Laufer, 1991, pp. 17-19; Kelly, 1986). Both implicit and explicit in this recognition is that such crime is committed by large criminal organizations, not single individuals or small groups of offenders. As will be described in the chapters ahead, such organizations involve much more than what is commonly understood as "organized crime."

To date there is no global criminal justice system to meet the challenge of globalized crime. The criminal justice systems of individual countries were not designed to meet such a challenge. Nation-states have only recently begun to comprehend the problem, as have academic criminologists. But awareness is rapidly developing (Adler, Mueller & Laufer, 1991). It has been said that the recent concern with terrorism on the world scene "marks the end of a narrow, parochial concept of corrections and law enforcement and places them in the more appropriate and broader perspectives of the political sciences" (Crelinsten, Laberge-Altmejd, & Szabo, 1978, p. xiii). The same would appear to apply to various other multinational crimes because of a variety of complex reasons arising out of the self-interests of the different nation-states involved. These self-interests can be simply described. Since many countries may profit economically and/or politically from at least some forms of multinational crime, the central government of none of these countries will easily commit itself to the control of *all* multinational crime. Each is likely to reserve the right to give the shelter of sovereignty, either directly or indirectly, to its own favored forms. Any future development of an effective international criminal justice system would, it seems, be required to function somehow within this powerful framework of dissent.

The concept of multinational systemic crime, sometimes called international or transnational crime, is now being discussed in the professional literature of criminology and criminal justice (see, for example, Bossard, 1990; Smith, 1989). Multinational systemic crime is, as already noted, more than an extension of domestic crime. It is crime by networks operating within a multinational arena, often with state support. While the motivation of individual participants within such networks may vary widely, the institutional purposes of these crime systems appear to be largely political or economic, or sometimes a combination of both. This suggests that a valuable frame of reference for describing and analyzing such crime systems is one that perceives their behavior as the political or economic behavior of organized private interest groups, or sometimes nation-states, or sometimes combinations of both, struggling on the world scene to achieve their own particular institutional goals. Perceived in this way multinational systemic crime is similar to, but a more extensive concept than "state-organized crime," as described by William J. Chambliss:

> The most important type of criminality organized by the state consists of acts defined by law as criminal and committed by state officials in the pursuit of their job as representatives of the state. Examples include a state's complicity in piracy, smuggling, assassinations, criminal conspiracies, acting as an accessory before or after the fact, and violating laws that limit their activities. In the latter category would be included the use of illegal methods of spying on citizens, diverting funds in ways prohibited by law (e.g., illegal campaign contributions, selling arms to countries prohibited by law, and supporting terrorist activities).
>
> State-organized crime does not include criminal acts that benefit only individual officeholders, such as the acceptance of bribes or the illegal use of violence by the police against individuals, unless such acts violate existing criminal law and are official policy. For example, the current policies of torture and random violence by the police in South Africa are incorporated under the category of state-organized crime because, apparently, those practices are both state policy and in violation of existing South African law. On the other hand, the excessive use of violence by the police in urban ghettos is not state-organized crime for it lacks the necessary institutionalized policy of the state. (Chambliss, 1989)[1]

State-organized crime differs from multinational systemic crime in that the former is always sponsored or directed by the state as a matter of official, but covert, policy; on the other hand, the latter may be entirely the activity of private organizations unrelated to any nation-state, except possibly through the corruption or other illegal activity of officials acting without the support of institutionalized state policy. Of the several multinational systemic crimes considered in this book, only the crime of espionage appears generally to be state-organized. The other crimes considered may or may not be state-organized, depending on the particular circumstances of a given case. In fact, in the secret and covert world of multinational systemic crime, a major difficulty confronting any investigation of such criminal activities is the determination of whether they are state-organized. The reason for this lack of clarity is, of course, one of design and purpose. The aim is to obscure and confuse. For this purpose a government intelligence agency, for example, may wholly own a "proprietary" concern, which is designed to provide some service and which appears in public as a private business. Or "front" organizations may be established whose purported business is a sham to provide cover for other activities. Or there might be an independent organization, established and operated on its own, but with close ideological ties with a government source, and many of the people who are employed by the organization are ex-employees of the same government source (Kwitny, 1987, pp. 120-121).

A nation-state undertakes to violate the law—either its own, or that of another nation-state, or both—through covert means in order to be able to deny culpability. One or more of the above three types of private organizations are used, plus other tactics of evasion. This adds a dimension to the study of multinational systemic crime not ordinarily encountered in the study of more conventional criminal behavior. Many ordinary crimes are complex, secret, and difficult to unravel, but only in state-supported crime are the massive resources of the nation-state available to hide the crime, obscure the facts, and deflect investigations (Kwitny, 1987).

Finally, it is significant to note that multinational crime often involves complex interactions between nation-states. In fact, such crime may constitute a significant mode of interaction in geopolitical affairs. Thus, such crime impacts the economic well-being, the foreign policy priorities, or even the national security of the nation affected. Moreover, while one or more nations may realize substantial gains from such conflict, some other nation or nations may endure substantial losses.

That such gains or losses may impact the economy, the foreign policy goals, or the national security of the nations involved escalates the political stakes participant nations have in how multinational crime is explained and what steps are accepted for its control. Thus, in a technical social science sense, national self-interests, measured in terms of a hierarchy of foreign or domestic policy goals, will sometimes substantially influence the very definitions national governments will accept with respect to multinational crime.

A very good illustration of this point is found in the argument presented in *The "Terrorism" Industry: The Experts and Institutions That Shape Our View of Terror* (Herman & O'Sullivan, 1989; see also Chomsky, 1988). In the judgment of Herman and O'Sullivan, this industry is also multinational, with close ties between government intelligence, military, and foreign policy agencies of the West and their allies, private sponsors, quasi-private think tanks, private security firms, and individual experts. Meeting and publishing regularly, these sources have established themselves as the accredited agents speaking out on the topic of terrorism for the Free World. Alternative or conflicting definitions of terrorism, frameworks of analysis, and policy judgments about control are excluded by these authorities for the West. This process of closure and exclusion has allowed management of the news about terrorism in the West, the molding of Western public opinion and public policy, and an ideological mobilization, all serving Western interests (Herman & O'Sullivan, 1989, pp. 8-9).

This "terrorism industry," Herman and O'Sullivan argue, has served the West very well as a cover for its own activities and crimes against the Third World as it has sought to maintain Western dominance. This has enabled the industry to label as "terrorism" both rebellion and national liberation movements in the Third World and to describe as legitimate "counterterrorism" the violence of the West and its client states to repress these conflicts (Herman & O'Sullivan, 1989, pp. 9, 218).

This analysis might be interpreted as an application to the field of international relations of what criminologists and others interested in less complex individual and group deviancy call "labeling theory" (see, for example, Vold & Bernard, 1986; Williams & McShane, 1988). In this case "big time" labeling is being applied across national boundaries by powerful agencies and spokesmen representing Western interests. To quote a classic statement by Howard Becker, "From this point of view, [terrorism] is *not* the quality of the act the person [or group] commits, but rather a consequence of the application by others of rules and sanctions. . . . The [terrorist] is one to whom that label has been successfully applied; [terrorism] is behavior that people so label" (Becker, 1963, p. 9). The same principle applies to the term *counterterrorism.* In the world of international affairs, an act of violence may be labeled as terrorism for one side; while, for the other, the act may be praised as a blow for national liberation.

If this same international interactions perspective were to be applied to other types of multinational crime, such as espionage, much the same sort of situation might apply. Thus, professional spies from one nation stealing military secrets from another might be labeled by the second nation as "serious threats to national security" and be imprisoned or executed if caught; at the same time, the same individuals might be celebrated as martyrs and heroes among their own people (see, for example, Raviv & Melman, 1990).

This duality of meaning for the deviant and for deviancy is a significant problem in the study and understanding of deviancy, including, it would seem, multinational crime. Especially lacking are studies that put the researcher in close contact with those he studies in their natural settings, so that he becomes fully aware of the people, their lives, and the reasons for their behavior. Much more available are studies based on so-called "objective" observations from sources outside of the world in which the deviant lives (Becker, 1963, pp. 168 ff.). The shortcomings of such studies from the "outside"—that is, outside the world of the deviant—are many, not the least of which is that they tend to omit the meaning of the interaction process between those who commit deviant acts and a variety of others (Becker, 1964), including possibly those against whom the behavior is directed.[2] If this interactionist approach on an international level could be applied more widely to the study of terrorism, espionage, and similar crimes, present understanding of these phenomena might be enhanced. At the very least, such research might serve in some small way to minimize the tendency to disregard certain variables in these problems because they are considered "distasteful" to researchers from some of the nation-states involved (Becker, 1964, pp. 4-6). When nations become caught up in the impact of what they label as *terrorism* and *drug-trafficking,* it is easy for their researchers to slip into what has been called the "conventional style" of focusing on the "deviants" themselves and ask questions mainly about them: Who is involved in these crimes? Where do they come from? How did they get that way (Becker, 1964, p. 2)? One obvious consequence of taking this approach to the study of multinational systemic crime is that the researcher, because he is so sharply focused on the deviants themselves, may fail to appreciate fully the larger regional or global context within which the behavior is occurring, specifically the variety of social interaction processes occurring between the various nations and other groups involved. As a result, this regional or global interaction may not be examined, and its relationship to the behavior in question may be unexplored.

A second consequence of looking mainly at individual deviants is that the systemic quality of their crimes may easily be slighted. Thus, in drug-trafficking for example, the criminal organizations involved may receive little consideration. Their names may be well known, such as in the case of the Medellín cocaine cartel, but little effort may be made to study such a criminal organization from the inside, in terms of its meaning for its participants, or to ascertain the variety and quality of its interactions with its various national and international social environments. So although the Medellín cartel may be very violent with its domestic and foreign enemies, at the same time it may have many friends and collaborators on the world scene, as well as in Colombia itself. But the behavior of the cartel may be best understood in terms of the definitions held by the actors involved inside the system. It is for this reason that criminal organizations themselves, as well as the various interactions of their participants as they encounter and define the succession of situations they confront, deserve direct empirical study (Blumer, 1969, pp. 6-7).

The emphasis on interaction in the study of multinational crime suggests the possible value of social and cultural conflict theories as an additional perspective useful in such study. Similar in some ways to labeling theory, conflict theories focus on the struggles for power and dominance as interactions between social groups and their cultures. Such theories assume that social life is much more characterized by conflict than by consensus. Regardless of their particular orientations to the sources of conflict in society and between societies, conflict theories view consensus as an aberration (Vold & Bernard, 1986, p. 96; Williams & McShane, 1988).[3] Nonetheless, social conflict is perhaps best perceived as only one of the social processes involved in the origin and development of the criminal organizations participating in multinational crime. Also likely to be involved are the social processes of cooperation, competition, and so on as the actors in such systems relate to each other and to their social environments. However, because law violation appears to be a core defining characteristic of many such systems, social conflict may be expected to play a significant role in influencing the culture and behavior of their participants, including increasing in-group solidarity and the formation of coalitions with other groups (Coser, 1956).

A brief and final note seems appropriate. Human groups and collectivities exist within social contexts and settings. It is proper to view and study such collectivities in terms of how participants make indications to themselves and to each other regarding how the collectivity should act in its area of operation (Blumer, 1969, p. 16). In specifying a model for the study of social conflict, Louis Kriesberg (1973, pp. 278-283) has called such areas of operation "settings." Such settings, according to Kriesberg (1973, p. 278), may be as various as nation-states, organizations, communities, and societies. It would seem that they may also include interdependent networks of nations linked through various forms of cooperation, such as trade, banking, and economic and military assistance. On the other hand, the relations between nations may be based essentially on hostility and conflict, as in the case of Israel and the Arab states. Whatever the content of the relationships between given nation-states, the relationships themselves and the nations involved would both appear to merit empirical study in their own right when they provide the contexts in which various criminal organizations carry on terrorism, arms-trafficking, and other types of multinational crime.

*   *   *

The book endeavors, in a very preliminary way, to break some ground in preparation for the eventual more rigorous study of multinational systemic crime from the perspective of interactionist and social and cultural conflict theories. It also emphasizes the value of studying the criminal organizations involved in such crime, as well as the regional and global settings in which they operate. Chapter 1 relates multinational systemic crime to the other major forms of crime studied by criminology and criminal justice. Chapters 2 and 3 describe four types of multinational crime (terrorism, espionage, drug-trafficking, and arms-trafficking) and comment on the place criminology and criminal justice occupy in the literature about these types. Chapter 4 comments on three observations that appear to be significant in the study of multinational crime: the apparent frequent interrelationship of such crimes on the international scene; the role of values, interests, and power in the study of such crimes and in policy formulations to control them; and the special role likely to be played by "national security" interests in limiting access to data needed for study of some forms of multinational crime. Chapter 5 identifies several problems in theory construction and policy development with respect to multinational systemic crime; also specified are some conceptual and methodological principles from the study of criminal organizations, from interactionist theory, and from conflict theory that appear useful for approaching the study of such crime. Chapter 6 describes three global regions that are significant for understanding much multinational systemic crime: the Golden Triangle of Southeast Asia; the Andean region of Colombia, Bolivia, and Peru; and the Middle East.

NOTES

1. For example, a description of an illegal arms/drug trafficking corporation (Kintex) organized by the Communist republic of Bulgaria is provided in Sterling (1990, pp. 158-163).

2. Blumer (1969) presents a classic statement of the interactionist point of view and its method.

3. Duke (1976) presents the major contributions to conflict theory by important social theorists. Kriesberg (1973) offers a framework for analyzing various kinds of social conflict. Sellin (1938) considers culture conflict theory as a structural source of crime.

1

Multinational Systemic Crime

For most of their history, academic criminology and criminal justice in the United States have concentrated their attention on crime as a domestic problem and on the studying of different aspects of the American criminal justice system. A similar domestic focus has also been the case in the study of crime and criminal justice in Great Britain, Germany, Japan, and other countries. From time to time some attention has also been given in various countries to cross-cultural or international studies, in which the crime patterns of different nations and their criminal justice systems have been compared with one another, using crime rates, cultural differences, contrasting sentencing practices, and so on.

Beginning in the 1970s criminologists and professionals in criminal justice began to take a serious interest in a variety of crimes by groups and organizations whose illegal activities transcend national boundaries. Such activities often originate and are directed from outside the jurisdictions of the legal systems of nation-states victimized by such networks. Because of their frequently clandestine nature and the fact that their operations may span continents, the effective control of such criminal networks by law enforcement is especially challenging. The object of this new focus in criminology and criminal justice may be called *multinational systemic crime,* a concept presented earlier in this volume.

DEFINITION OF MULTINATIONAL SYSTEMIC CRIME

Multinational means that such crime systems cross the jurisdictions, and impact or otherwise involve the social institutions and the citizens, of two or more nations; sometimes a dozen or more nations are involved. Such involvement is usually substantial and sustained, frequently for years.

An example of the large number of nations that may be involved in multinational crime systems is illustrated by the number reported to have been involved in the trafficking of heroin from Southeast Asia to Canada in the mid-1980s. Starting from the so-named Golden Triangle opium-growing area, the countries included: Thailand, Burma, Laos, China, Hong Kong, Malaysia, Taiwan, Korea, Japan, the Philippines, Singapore, India, Pakistan, Sri Lanka, Mexico, and the United States (Royal Canadian Mounted Police, 1988).

Systemic refers to the fact that such crime is the collective behavior of groups sometimes informally organized and at other times as formally organized as bureaucracies. Each group has its own leadership, division of labor, traditions, social norms, rewards, and sanctions. Such organizations may also have their own political constituencies and allied supporters; some may be state-sponsored.

Some of the continuity and organizational characteristics of such systems is illustrated in the following brief history of a West German terrorist group:

The killing of a leading West German banker by the precision bombing of his automobile near Frankfurt on November 30, 1989, was attributed to the Red Army Faction, which had its beginnings in the student protests of the 1960s. It was later established as the Baader-Meinhof Gang. In the early 1970s the group changed its name to the Red Army Faction and set out to topple through violence the social order in West Germany. The group received early training and logistical help from left-wing Palestinian groups. In 1977 Palestinian terrorists failed in their attempt to blackmail the West German government into freeing imprisoned leaders of the group by hijacking a Lufthansa plane to Somalia. Three leaders of the group then committed suicide simultaneously in West German prisons. The core of the group is estimated at no more than 30 people who actually conduct major attacks. This number is believed to be augmented by several hundred supporters. Since 1972 nine killings and violent assaults in West Germany, largely against ranking business executives, have been attributed to the group and related organizations.[1]

Crime refers to the fact that the behavior of such organizations is defined within the jurisdiction of at least one of the involved nations as a violation of its criminal code. It is most significant to note, however, that such criminal definitions need not be applied by each of the nations involved in multinational crime. Thus, for example, the U.S. Central Intelligence Agency has repeatedly shipped arms by air from Zaire to rebel forces in Angola. This may be legal in both Zaire and the United States, but it is almost certainly defined as illegal by the Marxist government of Angola. This government seized power back in 1976 when Portugal gave up after five centuries of colonial rule in Angola. The United States is the only major nation in the world not to have diplomatic relations with Angola, which since independence has received large amounts of aid from Eastern Europe, the Soviet Union, and Cuba. In early 1990 Cuba continued to maintain troops in Angola, and the United States continued to give about $50 million in annual military aid to Unita, a rebel group continuing to fight the independent government of Angola (Brooke, 1990b).[2] On May 31, 1991, the government of Angola and the rebels backed by the United States signed a peace treaty, which ended the 16-year civil war that took more than 300,000 lives. With this, the supply of weapons the United States had been sending to the rebels ended (Hoffman, 1991).

Such distinctions are historical ones in multinational systemic crime. Thus, for example, the smuggling of Indian-grown opium by British traders, and Turkish opium by their American counterparts, into China during the first half of the nineteenth century was legal according to British and American law. However, it was clearly criminal and vigorously, but ineffectively, opposed by the central government of China (Beeching, 1975; Chesneaux, Bastid, & Bergere, 1976; Fay, 1975).

In sum, multinational systemic crime may be defined as the behavior of ongoing organizations that involves two or more nations, with such behavior being defined as criminal by at least one of these nations.

THE IDENTIFICATION OF THE PROBLEM

During recent decades the news media have reported numerous instances of multinational terrorism, espionage, drug-trafficking, and arms-trafficking in various parts of the world. None was occurring for the first time. All were well documented previously in history. However, during the past 20 to 30 years new and dramatic outbreaks of each occurred. Different terrorist groups, some state-sponsored, took credit for hijackings, bombings, and assassinations; government-directed spy rings were uncovered; heroin and cocaine syndicates and cartels surfaced; and arms-trafficking by governments and private dealers was revealed. As a result, each of these criminal behavior systems, state-sponsored or not, received substantial publicity and attention as a major social and political problem, especially among Western nations. But control of these crimes usually proved to be most difficult. This difficulty arose in part from the fact that a precise understanding of the different clandestine, far reaching, and often fluid organizations carrying out these crimes was not readily available.[3]

The new outbreaks of the four criminal activities did not emerge for the same reasons, nor from the same sources. Moreover, they did not in recent years become defined as problems at one and the same time. In most recent years terrorism and espionage appear to have been identified as major international concerns earlier than modern drug-trafficking and arms-trafficking. Most of the literature about all four seems to have been written by historians, political scientists, journalists, intelligence specialists, and others outside the fields of criminology and criminal justice. Those two fields apparently first turned their attention to various global political and economic criminal organizations during the 1970s. There were observations made about the lack of concern criminology had shown for both the general topic of political crime and the many different kinds of international criminal networks.

Thus, in 1974 Stephen Schafer identified what he believed to be a serious omission in criminology. In discussing both domestic and international political crime, Schafer pointed out in a well-received book that: "Although political crime is the oldest and perhaps most recurring criminal phenomenon of history, and because of its impact by all means the most important, it has been largely ignored in criminological studies and has been the subject of little research or analysis" (Schafer, 1974, p. 8).

But in those days more than political crime was being omitted from criminology's agenda. Also being slighted were international networks of economic crime. Thus, in a significant statement about what he called "the crime industry," John A. Mack (1975) critically commented on the comparative neglect by criminologists of the study of mainly economically motivated, large-scale, international, criminal networks that include drug-trafficking and arms-trafficking within the scope of their activities.

At about the same time Manual Lopez-Rey (1974) addressed the differences between *conventional* (traditional) crime and what he termed *non-conventional* crime. Conventional crime is that committed by the "man in the street," which is usually dealt with by the police and the courts, and which usually involves persons of lower-status groups. Non-conventional crime includes offenses against international law; criminal law violations committed for patriotic, ideological, revolutionary, and similar reasons; crimes committed under the cover of official and semi-official governmental positions; and similar offenses. Lopez-Rey maintained that there is no clear and absolute division between the two concepts. He specifically identified terrorism, including state-sponsored terrorism, as a significant type of non-conventional crime. And most important for the purposes of this book, he concluded that although conventional crime was almost the exclusive concern of criminal justice systems and criminology, non-conventional crime was practically neglected by both.

As will be discussed in Chapters 2 and 3, the professional literature in criminology and criminal justice has given some attention to a detailed discussion of terrorism since at least the late 1970s. Starting in the mid-1980s, a few publications in those fields have also addressed drug-trafficking, but few if any publications have yet considered either espionage or arms-trafficking. By the end of the 1980s, terrorism and drug-trafficking had assumed a place in many textbooks on criminology, but espionage and arms-trafficking were seldom mentioned (see, for example, Adler, Mueller, & Laufer, 1991; Barlow, 1990; Gibbons, 1987; Meier, 1989; Reid, 1988).

In taking up the study of global criminal organizations, criminology and criminal justice have for perhaps the first time become interested in crime by nation-states committed against other nation-states. Certainly criminology has had a long-standing and productive interest in political corruption, police brutality, civil rights violations, and related crimes, but the new interest appears to be substantially different from these important domestic problems. It not only stresses the multinational nature of a variety of political and economic criminal organizations, but it also focuses increasingly on crimes committed by governments as part of their operating foreign policies. This dual focus has led to the identification of the need for, and a beginning recognition of the many political and legal difficulties associated with, the establishment of an efficient international criminal justice system, as discussed briefly in the Introduction. Thus, criminology and criminal justice may well be on the threshold of a new era if they continue to expand their emergent interests in multinational criminal organizations and their control. Much would seem to depend upon the interest and capacities of the two fields to apply productive and extensive research methods to the empirical study of such complex and usually powerful criminal organizations, to provide clear descriptions and interpretations of the structure and operations of such organizations in their different global settings, and to recommend effective measures of control tailored to meet relevant and varying conditions in different regions of the world.

But, as is discussed at greater length in Chapter 4, since crime control policy is seldom predicated simply on the conclusions set forth by social theory and research, acceptable recommendations for the control of multinational crime would have to be consistent with the relevant social values and political interests of the implementing nation-states. This would seem to suggest that in recommending policy to control multinational crime, it is as necessary to understand, in terms of ideological limits and political tolerance, the nature of the nation-states that would be expected to endorse and implement the policy, as it is to understand the nature of the criminal organizations targeted by the policy.

Perhaps some sense of the level of interest criminologists had in the topic of terrorism in the early 1980s is illustrated in the professional identifications of the contributors to a special issue of *The Annals of the American Academy of Political and Social Science* (September 1982), which was devoted to the subject of "International Terrorism." Although the editor of the issue was a well-known criminologist, very few of the 14 authors and co-authors of the articles in the issue were criminologists. Most were from the fields of political science, philosophy, or history, or from private defense and intelligence research institutes.

During the mid-1980s some comment was also made by professionals about the scarcity of studies concerning the international underworld of cocaine-trafficking. By this time much attention was being given in the news media and by public officials to the problem of global drug-trafficking. In this context, Edmundo Morales sought to make clear the essential distinction between the very popular study of drug addicts and addiction, and the very neglected study of systemic drug-trafficking. In 1986 he remarked about the poor state of the literature concerning international cocaine-trafficking:

> So far, the sociological and mental health aspects of cocaine have been the concern of social researchers and scholars. It is timely and long overdue to integrate the mechanics of production and the dynamics of distribution of cocaine in source countries and to look at the problem of drug abuse from a broader point of view. The political connotation of the international underworld should not be an excuse to exclude this important issue from scholarly practice. (Morales, 1986)

As will be made clear in Chapter 3, by the late 1980s, a growing literature about modern drug-trafficking was being published, often written by political scientists. By this time the smuggling of illegal drugs, especially from Third World heroin and cocaine source countries, to the nations of the West had become one of the most important crime problems faced by these industrialized regions. Clearly recognized as a world problem, drug-trafficking continued to resist effective control. Moreover, scientific knowledge about drug-trafficking systems in any organizational sense on an international scale appeared to be essentially absent from the professional literature of criminology and criminal justice, even as the last decade of the twentieth century began.

A similar situation seemed to exist with respect to a scientific understanding of terrorism, which was also recognized as a global problem. The sizable literature on the topic had yielded scant knowledge useful for the purposes of control. In a major paper about terrorism, M. Cherif Bassiouni (1981) pointed out that, although there had been numerous studies of terrorism in response to worldwide concerns, these studies lacked analytic consistency and failed to probe this phenomenon sufficiently. And, he continued, such studies did not seem to have influenced decision makers to formulate appropriate measures for effective prevention and control.

In the 1987 edition of his criminology text, Don C. Gibbons presents an insightful appraisal of the state of present knowledge about political crime, including terrorism. He concludes that criminology does not have a "surfeit"of well-developed theoretical statements about political crime. Further, a reading of his sections on terrorism appears to confirm Bassiouni's conclusion that terrorism has not been sufficiently studied to yield knowledge useful to decision makers interested in terrorism's prevention and control (Gibbons, 1987).

Nonetheless, despite these difficulties, since the 1970s a substantial expansion appears to have occurred in what might be called the "conceptual boundaries" of criminology and criminal justice. No longer is either constrained by a traditional focus on domestic crime and criminal justice. Major aspects of crime and its prevention and control are increasingly being defined in international or even global terms. Yet, this conceptual expansion beyond national boundaries and jurisdictions appears to be just beginning. Few answers exist with respect to multinational systemic crime, the focus of this book. In fact, few of the proper questions appear to have been asked. But the intellectual journey seems to have begun. As may be evident in the chapters that follow, this journey may well involve a much greater use by criminology and criminal justice of the theories and research methods of economics, cultural anthropology, and political science than has been common in the past.

MULTINATIONAL SYSTEMIC CRIME CONTRASTED WITH OTHER CATEGORIES OF CRIME

Criminologists and others who study crime in modern society often subdivide the general problem into various major categories, such as conventional crime, organized crime, white-collar crime, and so on. Figure 1.1 shows seven major categories of crime, including multinational systemic crime, and contrasts the categories in terms of two variables. The first relates to the relative degree to which each category involves systemic criminal behavior. The second relates to the relative degree to which the individuals or groups in each category are integrated with the economic, political, social, and other institutions of the larger society. The diagram suggests that the greater the systemic or organizational quality of the criminal activity and the greater the degree of integration with the social institutions of the larger society, the more efficient and powerful are likely to be the criminal actors and collectivities operating within each crime category. In sum, it may be hypothesized that the greater their organization and their integration with the institutions of the larger society, the greater the efficiency and power of the criminal elements involved in the various categories.

Thus, for example, conventional crime refers to the large bulk of domestic criminal law violations with which local, county, and state law enforcement agencies in the United States are primarily concerned. Such crime is typically the behavior of an individual or a small group of individuals who generally evidence little or no organization. Conventional criminals are often lower class and, hence, are poorly integrated with significant social institutions in the larger society, and consequently they have little power. Finally, conventional crime is the category of crime with which most local law enforcement agencies have the most experience and are most proficient in solving and successfully prosecuting.

At the other extreme, multinational systemic crimes, such as terrorism and espionage, are in almost all ways the direct opposite of everything that has been said regarding conventional crime. Multinational systemic crime is often statistically infrequent. It is often state-sponsored. It is typically well organized. Its significance to the public and to policy makers rests not so much in the frequency of its occurrence but in the provocative, fear-inducing, and genuine sense of threat such behavior represents to various organizations, both economic and political—up to and including nation-states.

Moving upward in the diagram away from conventional crime and toward multinational systemic crime, the criminal elements involved in the various categories may well become more efficient and more powerful through organization and social integration. One result is that such efficiency and power would seem to make their control by law enforcement agencies much more complex and difficult.[4] Moreover, the capacities of some of these criminal organizations to either corrupt or retaliate against the police, judges, jurors, witnesses, and others is historically legendary. Sometimes the retaliation is subtle but stinging; sometimes it is brutal and grossly violent. To go up against such power is frequently nerve-racking and sometimes even deadly. Witness the frequent bombings, kidnappings, and assassinations of police, military, judges, newspaper editors, and other targets in Lebanon, Northern Ireland, Colombia, Italy, Israel, and elsewhere. Increasingly of late the military has been called upon to support the police in the identification and suppression of some advanced forms of multinational systemic crime. This has introduced into criminal justice programs a major dimension and level of effort to control multinational crime not found in other categories of crime discussed in this chapter. A striking case in point was the December 1989 invasion of Panama by the U. S. Army in order to apprehend and bring to the United States for trial on drug-trafficking charges the head of government in Panama, General Manuel Antonio Noriega (Dinges, 1990; Kempe, 1990). It is perhaps significant to note here that less than two years after this military invasion to capture Noriega and to stamp out cocaine trafficking in Panama, cocaine was being shipped to the United States from Panama in even larger amounts than before Noriega's arrest. In his time

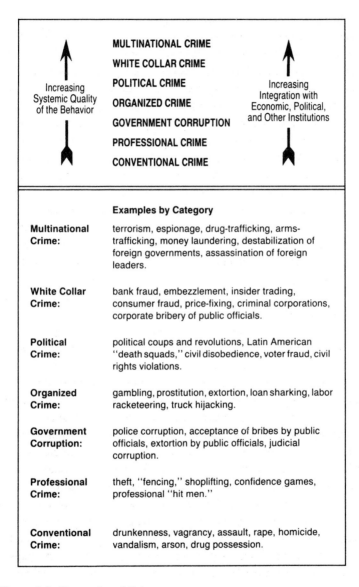

Figure 1.1. Categories of Crime

cocaine trafficking in Panama was an orderly affair. Since his removal, however, the illegal trade has boomed and became a free-for- all that is out of the control of the ineffective civilian government installed and sponsored by the United States (Treaster, 1991). From this it might be argued, at least in the short term, that the military invasion of Panama, the capture of Noriega, and his removal to the United States for trial have been counterproductive for America's War on Drugs.

Another illustration of the military's possible involvement in the suppression of multinational crime was found in 1990 in the reported planning of a large new United States military aid program to expand the drug war in Peru and to help that nation fight leftist guerrillas (Shining Path), who were said to protect coca growers and traffick- ers. The U.S. Army Special Forces would, according to the plan, train six Peruvian battalions for jungle warfare against the guerrillas. Amer- ican aid would also be given to Peru's air force and navy to assist in the war against drugs. It was anticipated that this new aid would supple- ment Peruvian and American helicopter teams already operating against the drug runners (Brooke, 1990b; Krauss, 1991; Nash, 1991).

Developments such as these, which involve American military operations within the territory of Third World nation-states, appear to be an application of what is reported to be a new assertive and com- prehensive U.S. military strategy for dealing with Third World prob- lems. The strategy, well planned and well thought out, is called "low intensity warfare." The use of military force by the United States, either overtly or covertly, to intervene in the affairs of other nation-states is scarcely new, especially in Latin America. What is new is that with the lessening of East-West tensions in Europe, there has apparently been a major concentration on building military intervention capacities to act against Third World revolutionary movements and governments. What is also new is the extension overseas of the military's domain into what is usually considered the function of the police.

The new proactive strategy explicitly identifies anti-drug opera- tions, rescue missions, punitive strikes, action against terrorism, and various other "mission categories" as part of the low-intensity con- flict that the United States military now performs. More than military power is involved. All elements of national power are to be applied, including covert political and psychological operations, and other "special activities." The description appears to be so deliberately broad and ambiguous that a wide range of activities is embraced. Thus, for perhaps the first time in United States history, the military has assumed an overseas police role as part of its new aggressive strategy for dealing with some forms of multinational systemic crime and other foreign threats to national security (Klare & Kornbluh, 1988).

Moreover, in November 1989 the Justice Department issued a 28-page memorandum to President Bush's National Security Adviser, ruling that the Posse Comitatus Act, which prohibits arrests by the military in the United States, does not apply abroad. Thus the military could now arrest drug traffickers and other fugitives overseas (Woodward, 1991, pp. 139-140).

Clearly if such American law enforcement activity by the military within the territory of another nation is done with that nation's approval, that is one thing. On the other hand, if such military intervention in the name of law enforcement is done without the target nation's approval, substantial issues of international law are raised, which, although essential to note here, are far too complex to be discussed here.[5]

The consequences such military developments could have for American criminal justice per se at present appear to be largely unexplored. What does appear clear is that any introduction of the United States military into an active police role overseas to control selected types of multinational crime would stand in sharp contrast with traditional law enforcement practices used to control various categories of domestic crime in the United States.

A variety of difficult and possibly unsettling questions for criminal justice may be asked about such a new overseas crime control policy: For example, might the military operating as police overseas have the same powers of interrogation, extended detention, and arrest on suspicion without evidence, as the British Army was reported to have in Northern Ireland in 1978 under The Prevention of Terrorism (Temporary Provisions) Act (Boyle, Hadden, & Hillyard, 1978; Crenshaw, 1987)? In the furtherance of such a policy, might United States military courts be empowered, under specific conditions, to try not only foreign nationals but also involved United States citizens? If the answers to these questions are affirmative, such a military justice policy might well result in a "military security" approach, of frequent arrest, interrogation, and detention with or without trial, being applied to populations suspected of certain multinational crimes overseas. This, of course, would contrast starkly with the civilian "police prosecution" approach to individual trial and proof of specific criminal acts that has long been traditional in the United States.[6]

Such substantial changes may, of course, never occur. Much depends on the course of future events. But the significant point seems to be that such changes in United States criminal justice would appear to be far more likely to occur in response to the threat of foreign-based multinational crime than they would be to arise because of the threat of almost any other category of crime discussed in this chapter. Only selected types of multinational crime appear at present to have a demonstrated capacity to be defined as threats to national security by the United States and other Western leaders. Of all the various categories of crime considered here, only drug-trafficking has repeatedly had a domestic and overseas "war" declared against it by the United States; only epi- sodic terrorism and threats of terrorism, as exemplified by the threats that occurred at the start of the Persian Gulf War in 1991, have triggered large-scale domestic security responses in the United States, Great Britain, and elsewhere, which generally have not been seen since World War II. Clearly, some modern forms of multinational systemic crime have a greater capacity to call forth an extraordinary national response in Western democracies than do most other categories of crime. In the case of terrorism, for example, almost inevitably such response is not limited to increasing the physical security of airports, government buildings, national leaders, and so on. It also often includes intelligence, law enforcement, and sometimes military activity, which offer powerful challenges to traditional civil liberties.[7]

NOTES

1. Adapted from Protzman (1989) and Throw, Aeppel, Mossberg, & Sesit (1989).
2. For a detailed description of early United States involvements in Angola during the 1970s, see Stockwell (1978).

3. For a description of the problems United States authorities experienced during the 1980s in discovering the existence of the powerful, large-scale, but diffuse Medellín cocaine cartel based in Colombia, see Gugliotta and Leen (1990). Moreover, as these authors report, once the concept of cocaine cartels was commonly accepted, there was wide disagreement among law enforcement officials about the structure and operations of such organizations.

4. For a discussion of significant differences in the political power bases of different types of career criminals and the relationships between power and immunity from prosecution, see Inciardi (1975).

5. For a discussion of the possibility that the United States is moving away from its strong historical support for international law, that it is perhaps beginning to define such law as optionally binding on its own actions, and that these changes are occurring as the nation becomes increasingly more powerful in the "new world order," see Moynihan (1990).

6. For a discussion of the differences between these two approaches to law enforcement, see Boyle, Hadden, & Hillyard (1978).

7. For a description of the extreme counterterrorism measures used by Israel, see Amir (1987).

2

Terrorism and Espionage

Four types of multinational systemic crime are considered in this chapter and in Chapter 3: terrorism, espionage, drug-trafficking, and arms-trafficking. The chapters also present case illustrations of such criminal systems. Such crimes, prominent in the news over the past two or three decades, have been of concern at the highest levels of government in the nations being victimized. Witness government responses to the violence of terrorism in Europe and the Middle East and to the threat of terrorism in the United States; the impact on public policy of cocaine and heroin importation into North America, Asia, Africa, Western Europe, and other areas of the world; and the violent consequences of forceful government action to bring drug kingpins to justice in Italy, Colombia, and Panama.

Such events are of a magnitude far beyond the usual social dislocation and concerns brought about by what was called "the crime problem" during earlier decades. Past crime in United States history has certainly been vexing and troublesome. Prohibition introduced a new level of organized violence to U.S. cities. Later larger-scale organized crime brought on new demands for crackdowns by law-enforcement. More recently white-collar crime has awakened serious concerns about crimes by corporations and by members of the privileged classes. And throughout the decades street crime and other conventional crimes have called forth repeated demands for vigorous police action. But no crime problem either inside or outside the United States appears to have competed with the sense of public threat exhibited during the past few decades over both the potential and the actual damage done by multinational systemic crime.

This chapter will consider terrorism and espionage. Chapter 3 will consider drug-trafficking and arms-trafficking.

TERRORISM

Some terrorism is domestic and some is multinational. All is politically motivated behavior. Politically motivated domestic violence has long been characteristic of American society; frequently such violence has been called "terrorism" (Kittrie & Wedlock, 1986). Some of the Victorian roots of the modern British Secret Intelligence Service, for example, are found in the establishment within Scotland Yard during the early 1880s of a Special Irish Branch to counter the Irish rebel bombings of British cities (Andrew, 1986, pp. 15-20). Today's press continues to report on the bombings and other violence that mark current phases of the continuing political struggle over "the Irish question" in Britain.

Nineteenth- and early twentieth-century Russian and Eastern Europe had well-established traditions regarding the use of systematic tactical terror for the accomplishment of political ends; these patterns continued into contemporary times. Much of this early terror became institutionalized as a kind of political style carried on by professional leaders and parties. Such terror became a way of doing political business, and as such it was totally foreign to the Western concept of the democratic transfer of power through majority rule (Gross, 1969). On the other hand, recent U.S. domestic terrorism has been much more episodic and has resulted in little loss of life. It has involved small indigenous groups, such as the Black Liberation Army, the Weather Underground, the Cuban Nationalist Movement, and the Justice Commandos for the Armenian Genocide.

Over the past 30 or 40 years, Puerto Rican Nationalist groups have been among the most active and persistent of the politically violent domestic groups in the United States. Nonetheless, domestic terrorism in the United States has not been generally defined as a major threat to the security of the nation. But this is not the case with American interests and citizens overseas. Here, multinational terrorism against various targets has seriously harmed U.S. interests and has injured or killed U.S. citizens, as well as those of other nations. Particularly in Africa, Europe, the Middle East, and Latin America, multinational terrorism by quasi-independent groups, often apparently equipped, trained, and given sanctuary by various national governments, is being directed at foreign political targets. At the same time, a number of politically violent groups, such as the Palestine Liberation Organization, the Irish Republican Army, the African National Congress, and various death squads in Latin America have, matured into self-sustaining organisms, each group learning from the others. Presently loose confederations of groups, often labeled "terrorist," appear to operate without the loss of autonomy that centralized control would impose (Kupperman, 1985).

Definition of Terrorism

There are a number of definitions of terrorism, including the one that views it as:

> A type of political crime that emphasizes violence as a mechanism to promote change. Whereas, other political criminals may engage in acts such as demonstrating, counterfeiting, selling secrets, spying, and the like, terrorists make systematic use of murder and destruction or the threat of such violence to terrorize individuals, groups, communities, or governments into conceding to the terrorists' political demands. (Siegel, 1986, p. 321)

But the matter of a definition of terrorism is not simple. David Long, in his *The Anatomy of Terrorism* (1990, pp. 3-4, 7), points out quite correctly that although scores of definitions of terrorism have been created, we are still nowhere close to a universally accepted definition of the term. The principal obstacle has been and continues to be that different nations have different political self-interests when it comes to responding both to events of political violence and to the groups that commit them. This makes the problem of developing an international consensus about the meaning of terrorism exceedingly difficult. Moreover, terrorism per se is often not a criminal offense in specific jurisdictions, so law enforcement agencies focus on specific and well-defined criminal acts committed by terrorists as part of their political operations. Such acts include, but are not limited to, murder, assault, hijacking, kidnapping, arson, and sabotage.

Long points out that there are also semantic problems with developing a commonly accepted definition of terrorism. Distinctions are made between terrorism and other forms of political violence, such as nuclear, chemical, biological, and guerrilla warfare, as well as revolutions and rebellions. Distinctions are also made between terrorism and such nonpolitical crimes as murder, hijacking, and kidnapping; however, a consensus is also lacking about what these distinctions should be.

Literature About Terrorism

Yet despite these difficulties (and perhaps in part because of them), there is a considerable literature about terrorism, much of it empirical, which has existed since at least 1910, a literature written primarily by those outside the fields of criminology and criminal justice (Romano, 1984). Using more than 100 references published since 1960, Reuben Miller summarized much of the recent literature on terrorism in an article that appeared in *Terrorism: An International Journal* (11:1, 1988). He found two main types of studies of terrorism, each with two or more subtypes:

Traditional Studies. These isolate a few cases of terrorism for analysis: Historical studies, which ask "Who are the terrorists? Why have the acts of terrorism been employed?" Such studies trace the ideology and actions of terrorists.

Normative studies, which focus on legal and judicial aspects of international terrorism. Here the focus is on terrorism as a criminal act and on its relations with international law.

Behavioral Studies. These attempt to explain terrorism in a systematic and scientific fashion, suggesting ways for societies to cope with the threat of terrorism:

Psychological studies, which seek to determine a psychiatric "terrorist personality" or profile. Here attention is also given to the personality dynamics of individual terrorists, and research here has concentrated on the small-group dynamics of terrorist groups.

Socioeconomic studies, which deal with political and social violence that encompass terrorism: What are the roots of these conflicts whereby some groups and some countries experience intense political violence while others do not? What are the patterns of internal conflict? Efforts are made to explain the environment of terrorism by examining the causative effect of economic, historical, cultural, and similar variables.

Public policy studies, which have not traditionally focused on terrorism, but instead have examined such mainstream domestic policy areas as health services, education, environment, housing, income, taxation, welfare, and so on. At the same time, because of the failure of the international community to cooperate and coordinate operations to counter terrorism, governments have acted on their own. Therefore, international terrorism has fallen into a gray area between domestic and foreign policy analysis. In the United States, international terrorism has generated an abundance of public documents from congressional hearings and so forth, but public policy writings have given slight attention to the phenomenon. The few works that have focused on the problem have not examined the relationship between government policies and terrorist activity; and such works remain speculative and prescriptive.

Other Studies

It is in error, of course, to conclude either that terrorists themselves, as distinguished from terrorism as a form of violence, have not been studied or that they have not been available for study. The work of Reuben Miller summarized above clearly specifies that various psychological studies done on individual terrorists represent a significant part of the literature on terrorism. This is reaffirmed by another analysis of the literature on terrorism, which revealed that terrorists themselves have been intensively investigated through the use of individualistically oriented conceptual schemes. Thus, Romano found, in her analysis of the literature on terrorism since 1910, a variety of interpretations emphasizing that terrorists suffered from different types of psychogenic and biological defects (Romano, 1984, p. 2). For example, two American psychiatrists, David Hubbard of the Aberrant Behavior Center in Dallas, and F. Gentry Harris of San Francisco, examined 80 imprisoned terrorists in 11 countries and found that 90% of them gave clear clinical evidence of defective vestibular functions of the middle ear (Romano, 1984, p. 6). Still other psychiatrists have found that terrorists were the products either of overpermissive families or of healthy superior families with whom they were in conflict, or they were victims of inconsistent mothering and isolation from the family (Romano, 1984, p. 36).

In recent years criminologists and professionals in criminal justice have also studied terrorism. Their publications include:

John D. Elliott and Leslie K. Gibson (Eds.), *Contemporary Terrorism: Selected Readings* (1978). Published by the International Association of Chiefs of Police, this collection of 20 previously published articles begins with the admonition that the best policy for governments to follow in dealing with terrorists is one that insures that no bargaining should occur with them. The editors urge that for a government to succumb to terrorist demands is to invite repeated attacks. They also note that terrorism is becoming increasingly state-sponsored and international, and that there is growing direct cooperation among nations in responding to such violence.

The various articles discuss, among other things, the history and power of terrorism, the high threat potential of such contemporary violence, and modern state-supported terrorist networks; national responses to terrorism and hostage taking, the value of intelligence, and a policy of deterrence are also highlighted. Statistical analyses of terrorist incidents and a statistical description of some characteristics of terrorists, their recruitment, and their presumed political philosophies are also provided.

Ronald D. Crelinsten, Danielle Laberge-Altmejd, Denis Szabo, *Terrorism and Criminal Justice: An International Perspective* (1978). Derived from a conference titled "The Impact of Terrorism and Skyjacking on the Operations of the Criminal Justice System," this book maintains as its most consistent theme that the criminal justice system should deal with terrorism in the same way that it deals with all other important crimes. Uniquely designed operations to combat terrorism—counterterrorist squads, special courts, discriminatory sentencing, and so on—usually cause more problems than they solve. The authors also point out that the popular tactic of target-hardening, although it has been effective in such areas of skyjacking, cannot be expected to prevent future terrorist activities as long as no effort is made to provide legitimate means to redress the grievances of terrorists when they in fact exist. Last, the authors raise, but do not attempt to settle, the issue of legal jurisdiction in incidents of international terrorism.

The second half of the book presents a comparative description of the impact of terrorism in the United States and six European countries.

Austin T. Turk, *Political Criminality: The Defiance and Defense of Authority* (1982). This is a most significant theoretical statement about political crime, in which the author stresses among other things the need to distinguish between political crime and political policing. Political *crime* refers to those behaviors that are defined by authorities as real threats to their welfare and to the welfare of the societies they represent; political *policing* refers to the illegal and other activities of authorities aimed at the repression of those they perceive as threats to the social order. Quite clearly, the term *terrorism* has been applied to some of the violence found in political crime, as well as to some of that found in political policing. One illustration of the latter is the 1964-1979 domestic reign of terror in Brazil, undertaken systematically by military governments to protect what was deemed to be "national security" (Wright, 1986).

Nicholas N. Kittrie and Eldon D. Wedlock, Jr., (Eds.), *The Tree of Liberty: A Documentary History of Rebellion and Political Crime in America* (1986). "The terms *political crime* and *political criminals* are rarely found in the American literature of the social and political sciences, history, criminology, or law." With this statement the authors begin their detailed history of political crime, both violent and nonviolent, in America, dating back to the earliest European settlers, and carry their history forward until August 8, 1985, when the federal International Terrorism and Foreign Airport Security legislation was approved.

The authors trace domestic terrorism in the United States back to the Haymarket Square bombing in Chicago in 1886 (document 163); and to the violence of a white vigilante group against black citizens and black government officials in Wilmington, North Carolina, in 1898 (document 172). They trace American public concern regarding modern international terrorism back to international aircraft hi-jackings and congressional amendments in 1961 to the Federal Aviation Act of 1958, thereby creating the new crime of "air piracy" (document 380).

Richard H. Ward and Harold E. Smith (Eds.), *International Terrorism: The Domestic Response* (1987). (See also Buckwalter, 1989; Ward & Smith, 1988). Most of the 16 articles in this book were presented at a conference called "International Terrorism: The Domestic Threat." A recurring theme in the book is the deep and ongoing strain felt in democratic societies when needs for national security through counterterrorism activities clash with the normal restraints usually imposed on police activities. Carefully reviewed are the problems and negative consequences of efforts to define terrorism as a distinct criminal act, including the absolute need to keep the motivational aspects of terrorism separate from the legal issues of crimes and violence. In definitions of crime, the issue is (or should be) behavior, *not* motivation, be it political, economic, vindictive, or so on.

But the central emphasis of this collection of articles is on the shock and impact various "special" counterterrorism measures have on civil liberties when and if they are imposed in democratic societies. By name these measures include but are not limited to: proactive intelligence investigations, preventive detention, civilian trial before military courts, assassinations of designated terrorist leaders, and military operations against terrorist targets in civilian areas.

Counterarguments presented include statements that such counterterrorism measures are only temporary, that they are monitored regularly by trustworthy officials, and that they are necessary for national security or even survival.

Several observations seem appropriate regarding the above five publications. First, from the perspective of theory and research, the five do not present very much empirical data about the biographies of today's terrorists; moreover, there is almost no empirical data presented about the internal workings of terrorist organizations and their international networks, or the structural and functional links between such networks and the nation-states that are presumed to be supporting them.

Second, there is very little information about the precise motivations of terrorists and the goals of their organizations, measured in terms of specific grievances when they do exist. If terrorism is a kind of low-intensity warfare between nations or sub-national groups, what is the war about? Who wants precisely what? There are very few answers to such questions in the publications examined.

Last, there appears to be little suggestion about the specifics of the empirical research methodologies, which, when applied to the study of terrorism, terrorists, their social organizations, and the social conflict in which they are engaged, are likely to yield an understanding of terrorism as experienced by its participants, of terrorists as functioning human beings, of the structure and function of their organizations, and whether the conflict in which they are engaged can be subjected to any kind of accommodation or resolution. There is also very little information about the history, culture, politics, economics, and religion of the environments or settings out of which terrorism emerges and within which terrorist organizations operate.

CASE MATERIAL ABOUT TERRORISM

Bombing for Iran:
Political Crime Between Nations

The following news item describes multinational terrorism carried out in France in the mid-1980s by a 20-person terrorist network, led by a Tunisian-born Frenchman, who was said to have belonged to the Beirut-based Party of God, a pro-Iranian militia. Other systemic qualities of the case, such as recruitment and training, are clearly evident.

Paris, Jan. 29—A major terrorism trial opened here today when a tribunal began examining a case involving the 20-person terrorist network allegedly organized by Fouad Ali Saleh, who is said to have belonged to the Beirut-based Party of God, a pro-Iranian militia.

After a three-year investigation, Mr. Saleh, a 31-year-old Tunisian-born Frenchman, has been identified by the French authorities as the "master-mind" behind 15 bombings and attempted bombings that left 13 people dead and nearly 250 people wounded in Paris in 1985 and

1986. He is said to have studied in Iran and received training in the use of explosives in Lebanon.

Nine other people are being tried with Mr. Saleh, including his wife, Karima Ferahi, a French woman of Algerian descent. The defendants are accused of possession and transportation of explosives and of planning and executing the bombings over a nine-month period. The bombs were set off in Paris train stations, department stores and other public places, including the Eiffel Tower. The authorities say that the group carried out the bombings to discourage France from supplying Iraq with weapons during its eight-year war with Iran.

Shouts Insults at Prosecutor

Shortly after the trial began, the presiding judge ordered Mr. Saleh ejected from the courtroom for proclaiming loudly, "My name is Death to the West!" and "War, holy war!" in a harangue that continued for nearly five minutes. He accused the French of having killed 2 million Algerians during Algeria's war of independence in the 1950s and 1960s. When asked to be silent, Mr. Saleh refused. "You are posing as great lords and the only way to make you crack is explosives!" the French news agency quoted him as saying. The judge sentenced him to a year in jail for contempt of court and ordered him taken back to his cell. Eight Lebanese are to be tried in absentia on the same charges. These men, who are all believed to be in Lebanon, are said to be members of the Party of God. In this trial, the accused face the charge of possession of explosives, which carries a sentence of 10 to 20 years. The same defendants will be tried for murder later this year.

Links to Terrorist in TWA Case

According to the prosecution, the defendants were arrested as they were replenishing their stock of explosives with new shipments from Lebanon. Mr. Saleh's name was first spotted in an address book carried by Mohammed Ali Hamadei, a Party of God terrorist who was arrested in Germany in January 1987.

Mr. Hamadei was carrying explosives and presumably was on his way to France. He was sentenced to life in prison last May in West Germany for his participation in the 1985 hijacking of a TWA airliner to Beirut. An American was beaten and shot to death during the hijacking. French officials said that in addition to the Party of God operatives, their investigation implicates some senior Iranian officials, including a former Interior Minister, Ali Akbaar Mohtashemi, now a member of the Iranian Parliament. Mr. Saleh, who was arrested in March 1987, has reportedly refused to cooperate with the police or the examining magistrate in the case. Much of the information obtained in the investigation came from an informer and the French counterespionage and counter-terrorism services.

Embittered by Racism

The informer, once an associate of Mr. Saleh, received a reward of about $178,000 and was released in return for his help in the arrest and prosecution of Mr. Saleh. He traveled later to the United States to provide information to American anti-terrorist agencies, French officials say, and has since returned to Tunisia.

According to investigators, Mr. Saleh, who was known to his accomplices as Ali al-Tunsi, or Ali the Tunisian, was deeply embittered by what he viewed as racism toward Arabs in France. With few prospects of employment in Tunisia, Mr. Saleh became fascinated by the preachings of Ayatollah Ruhollah Khomeini, the leader of the revolution that deposed Shah Mohammed Riza Pahlevi in 1979.

In 1980, according to investigators, he traveled to Iran, where he studied for two years in the religious seminaries of Qom, the Shiite holy city where most of Iran's clergy receive their religious instruction.

Although not much is known about his experiences in Iran, French investigators say that Mr. Saleh returned to France in 1983 with his devotion to Ayatollah Khomeini and the Iranian Government reinforced. He converted from Sunni Islam to Shiite Islam and began to proselytize, preaching in public places on weekends and in private to friends, most of whom were poor Arab immigrants from North Africa. He made a meager living selling fruits, vegetables and clothes in the Paris subway.

Reportedly Trained in Lebanon

He was spotted preaching by agents of the Lebanese Party of God and was recruited soon afterward, the investigators said. He traveled to Beirut, where he was trained to carry, conceal, and manufacture explosives, and, finally, to plan bombings that would do enough damage to dissuade France from supplying arms to Iraq. (Ibrahim, 1990).

ESPIONAGE[1]

Espionage is perhaps the oldest of the multinational crime systems considered in this book. Espionage is a crime that is both political and, because it typically involves two or more nations, multinational.

Throughout history it has usually been recognized as a serious offense, frequently punished by either lengthy terms of imprisonment or death. Sometimes convicted spies are also heavily fined. Needless to say, even when they are first offenders, they are seldom placed on probation or assigned to community service.

As a source of intelligence about foreign lands and their peoples, spying dates back to at least the time of Moses (Andrew, 1986, p. 1). Modern espionage is perhaps the most sophisticated and clandestine of the four crime systems being considered. Little is actually known about it by the public, except for what appears in the press and popular literature about a relatively few exposed spies on the domestic scene, or is presented in the literature about the operations of the complex intelligence networks of various nations, such as the American CIA (Ranelagh, 1986; Rositzke, 1977) and the Soviet KGB (Corson & Crowley, 1985).

Today there is a very substantial nonfiction literature in English on the subject of espionage. During the past decade or so, this literature has increased rapidly as public interest in spies and espionage mounted during what some have called "the decade of the spy." A 1983 analytical bibliography of intelligence and espionage publications (George C. Constantinides, *Intelligence and Espionage: An Analytical Bibliography*) presented in-depth descriptions and evaluations of some 500 English-language nonfiction books on the subject. Among the many events and time periods covered in the bibliography were the American Revolution, the Civil War, World War I, the Bolshevik Revolution, the rise of the Soviet Union, World War II, and the postwar era.

This bibliography and a survey of English-language nonfiction books on espionage published after 1980 indicate that nonfiction books on espionage have been published by historians, journalists, military and intelligence analysts, ex-spies, and a variety of others. But few if any of the authors have been academic criminologists.

Espionage as a Systemic Crime

Most public images of spies view them as either lone individuals or small groups working secretly and in isolation to steal a nation's secrets and to hand them over to the enemy. When it comes to espionage, the public tends to see the tip of the iceberg, not the vast mass of ice that floats in secret below the surface. Far from being a crime committed by lone individuals or small groups, espionage between modern nation-states is a large-scale activity carried out by complex bureaucracies. The following sections will present a brief theoretical orientation useful for conceptualizing espionage as a systemic crime.

It is reported by Allen and Polmar that as late as the 1950s, U.S. counter-espionage strategy focused on individual Americans as spies rather than on their spymasters. A few American counter-espionage agents following this strategy were no match for the worldwide Soviet espionage apparatus that commanded lavish resources and all the skilled people it needed from its own government. It was an uneven contest, a handful of American agents against a large Soviet apparatus (Allen & Polmar, 1988, p. 39).

Allen and Polmar also present a list of 94 individuals involved in espionage against the United States since the 1950s: 43 United States servicemen, 18 federal employees, 6 defense contractor employees, as well as 27 foreign agents. The list of foreign agents does not include the so-called "legal" diplomatic spies who were simply expelled from the United States. Each of the four categories is illustrated below:

United States Servicemen

Army Sergeant Jack F. Dunlap, assigned to the National Security Agency, committed suicide in 1963. After his death it was discovered that he had been a Soviet spy. The extent of his spying has never been revealed.

Lieutenant Colonel William H. Whalen, an Army intelligence officer stationed at the Pentagon, sold secrets to the Soviets. Arrested in 1966, he was sentenced to 15 years in prison.

John Walker, a Navy warrant officer and communication specialist who spied for the Soviets for at least 17 years, was arrested in 1985; he was sentenced to life imprisonment.

Federal Employees

Sharon M. Scrange, who was recruited to spy for Ghana while working there for the CIA, was sentenced in November 1985 to 5 years. In May 1986 this was cut to 2 years, with a recommendation for parole in 18 months.

Larry Wu-Tai Chin, who had spied for China while he worked for the CIA, was convicted of espionage. While awaiting what could have been a life sentence, he was found dead in his cell, apparently a suicide, on February 21, 1986.

Richard W. Miller, an FBI agent, was convicted of engaging in espionage with a Soviet emigre. Arrested in 1984, he was sentenced to life imprisonment.

Defense Contractor Employees

William Holden Bell, a Hughes Aircraft employee, sold secrets of several projects to a representative of the Polish Intelligence Services. Arrested in 1981, he was sentenced to 8 years in prison.

Randy Miles Jeffries, a messenger for a company that transcribed congressional hearings, in 1985 gave some classified documents to a Soviet official and later attempted to sell others to an FBI agent posing as a Soviet intelligence officer. Jeffries pleaded guilty to one count of espionage and received a 10-year sentence.

Foreign Agents

Rudolf Ivanovich Abel, a Soviet "illegal," operated in the United States in the 1950s. Arrested in 1957, he was sentenced to a total of 45 years on three counts. In February 1962 he was exchanged for Francis Gary Powers, pilot of a U-2 spy plane shot down over the Soviet Union, who had spent 18 months in a Soviet prison as a spy.

Otto Attila Gilbert, a naturalized U.S. citizen, spied for his native Hungary. Arrested in 1982, he was sentenced to 15 years.

Marian Zacharski, an officer of the Polish Intelligence Service, was convicted of espionage in 1981 and given a life sentence. In 1985 was swapped, along with three other spies from Eastern Bloc countries.

Gennardi F. Zakharov, a Soviet scientist employed by the United Nations, was arrested on August 23, 1986. He pleaded no contest in court and was allowed to return to the Soviet Union in a deal that also saw the release of American reporter Nicholas Daniloff, who had been arrested as a spy in Moscow in retaliation for the Zakharov arrest.

Granting the accuracy of the observation by Allen and Polmar presented above that individual spies should not be studied in isolation from their spymasters, it would appear that espionage should not be viewed as the single act or even the repeated acts of particular individuals who are motivated by greed, ideology, revenge, or being blackmailed; or of small groups, as is frequently the case in many other types of crimes such as embezzlement, rape, robbery, breaking and entering, check forgery, and income tax evasion. Instead, espionage should be conceptualized as a type of systemic or organizational crime in which individual spies participate for various reasons. Some are professionals, others are motivated by greed, ideology, or revenge. Still others are entrapped or blackmailed by foreign intelligence agencies. Whatever the motivations of individual spies, each functions as a foreign intelligence source for a foreign power. From this perspective espionage involves a hierarchical system of social status and social roles, the purpose of which is to transfer information harmful to the national interests of one nation-state to another, which may or may not be hostile to the nation-state from which the information is purloined. Espionage operations between hostile nation-states may go on for decades, even generations. For present purposes espionage systems operating against the interests of the United States will be viewed in light of the three following components:

(1) the actual behavior for which individuals may be charged under Title 18, Chapter 37, Sections 792 through 799 of the U.S. Code;[2]
(2) the social, cultural, and personality characteristics of such individuals;
(3) the foreign intelligence organizations that recruit, encourage, and control the espionage activities of such individuals.

In more detail, espionage systems may be conceptualized as involving the following status-role hierarchy. This hierarchy is but part of the much larger intelligence agency bureaucracy of modern nation-states. In this espionage hierarchy, control and direction flow downward while information from "target" nation-states is passed upward. At the top of the hierarchy are the executives of espionage systems. There are the *officers* of various national intelligence agencies (such as the KGB and the CIA). Some of these may stay at home in their own national capitals while more junior officers are sent as *legals* or *illegals* into the target nation. Legals may be sent as diplomats to control and recruit personnel. They are seldom directly active in spying, but serve as *case-officers* or *controllers*. Illegals are sent to the target nation, but operate under deep cover with false identities and a *legend* (fictitious life history). They may also serve as case-officers or controllers. *Spy-masters* are super controllers who run several *assets* or a *spy ring* in the target nation.

Assets and similar personnel are *agents* of their parent foreign intelligence organization. It is through their controllers that they both receive direction and pass their information upward for analysis and evaluation. Agents come in various forms: *penetration agents* are *moles* who work under deep cover and well inside the established significant institutions of the target nation, such as that nation's espionage and defense establishments; *double agents* who work for both sides; *auxiliary agents*, including *cut-outs* or other intermediaries; and *feed-back agents* who provide running commentaries on events and operations in target nations and who may be *stay-behinds*, that is, agents who are left in place in areas abandoned by retreating troops or armies during wartime. *Agents of influence* are under less direction, and sometimes no direction at all, from spy-system controllers. They are hidden persuaders, including politicians, diplomats, civil servants, trade union leaders, academics, journalists, and clergy, who function from within their target nation to influence public opinion and decisions favorable to a foreign power. In the context of espionage systems, agents of all types are expendable and replaceable. The systems, however, go on (Pincher, 1987).

The American Intelligence Community and Espionage

Every modern nation-state has its own intelligence community composed of its designated intelligence agencies. The primary purpose of intelligence agencies is to gather information about other nations which will be useful to the policy makers of their own nations. Much of the information gathered is public, but intelligence agencies especially seek information that other governments try to conceal.

John Macartney (1988) describes the highly bureaucratic intelligence community of the United States in the following terms. Intelligence is a staff, not a line function and, hence, the community is a loose conglomeration of agencies working under the coordination and guidance of the Director of Central Intelligence and his intelligence community staff. The DCI is also director of the independent Central Intelligence Agency, as well as the President's Intelligence Adviser. Except for the President, and increasingly the Congress, no one holds direct command over the whole community. Coordination is obtained through a web of interagency committees and staffs, rather than through a chain of command.

The CIA is unique in the U.S. intelligence community because it is autonomous, rather than a staff element of a larger government department. The agency has the biggest analytical staff within the community and also exercises primary national responsibility for the clandestine collection of human intelligence. Additionally, and uniquely, the CIA is also charged with conducting approved covert action missions.

The National Security Agency, headquartered at Ft. Meade, Maryland, is part of the Defense Department. It is responsible for communications security as well as collecting, processing, and disseminating signals intelligence. Each of the military services also has sizable signals intelligence elements that are coordinated and managed by NSA.

The Defense Intelligence Agency, located at Bolling Air Force Base in Washington, D.C., is a joint defense agency that serves the foreign intelligence requirements of the Secretary of Defense, the Joint Chiefs of Staff, and the United and Specified Commands. The DIA provides all types of finished intelligence, but its specialty is military intelligence. The Director of DIA is also Director of Military Intelligence and Intelligence Deputy for the JCS. The DIA also manages the worldwide Defense Attache System and provides a number of services to the intelligence community, including photo processing and operation of the Defense Intelligence College. The Director of DIA also coordinates the intelligence activities of the four military services, with facilities and personnel scattered worldwide throughout the operating commands of the Army, Navy, Air Force, and Marine Corps.

The Departments of State, Treasury, and Energy have intelligence elements that are much smaller than either the Central Intelligence Agency or the Department of Defense intelligence arms.

The Federal Bureau of Investigation has domestic counterintelligence responsibilities, and its counterintelligence arm is part of the intelligence community, unlike its criminal division and other law enforcement elements.

Of all the agencies making up the intelligence community, the clandestine gathering of human intelligence against foreign government targets (espionage) is the primary responsibility of the CIA. Typically this involves case officers and agents, who are generally foreigners.

Counterintelligence is the activity conducted and the information gathered to protect the United States against foreign espionage, other clandestine intelligence activities, sabotage, and terrorism. Within the United States, the FBI has overall responsibility for counterintelligence, while the CIA has primary responsibility abroad. The military services also have counterintelligence capacities.

Clandestine human intelligence activity and counterintelligence make up the world of espionage and counterespionage, of spymasters and spies, of defectors and double agents. When those spying against the United States are caught, if they are diplomats of a foreign country they may either be expelled or fed disinformation. If not diplomats, they may be turned into double agents or be subjected to criminal prosecution.

This then is a brief overview of the American intelligence community, as described by John Macartney, and the place of espionage within it.[3] Espionage is always considered a serious criminal offense by the nation against which it is directed. There is, of course, a good deal of literature about spies and spying, both against the national security interests of the United States and against the interests of other nations by the United States and other countries (see, for example, Knightley, 1986; Prange, Goldstein, & Dillon, 1984; Wise, 1988; Wright, 1987).

Perhaps the most significant fact to be gleaned from this literature for present purposes is that espionage against the United States or by the United States against a foreign power is not simply the work of a single spy or even of small groups of spies. Rather it is a complex criminal activity against a nation-state, involving the close and intensive support and direction by the intelligence bureaucracy of another nation-state, as exemplified by the American intelligence community described above. Of course, not all parts of such a community are equally involved in directing the work of one foreign agent, or even several. In fact, for reasons of security, the very existence of a particular foreign agent may be known to only a very few people. Nevertheless, the agent is an asset of the intelligence parent bureaucracy, which receives, evaluates, and makes use of the information the agent provides to his case officer supervisor, usually within the context of a larger stream of information obtained from various other sources. This relationship between the spy, the spymaster, and the sponsoring nation-state may go on for years. It is for these reasons that espionage in this book is considered to be a type of multinational systemic crime.

CASE MATERIAL ABOUT ESPIONAGE

A Long-Time Russian Traitor

The intricacies of espionage and counterespionage between modern nation-states are illustrated in the following news report about a long-time Russian diplomat who spied for the United States and was caught in the Soviet Union and sentenced to death.

MOSCOW, Jan. 14—A senior Soviet diplomat who for almost 30 years passed defense secrets to United States intelligence has been sentenced to death in Moscow.

It is not clear whether the sentence has been carried out.

The Communist Party newspaper Pravda today outlined the remarkable career of a man it identified only as Donald, whose exploits it said had included secret radio transmissions to the United States Embassy from a passing Moscow trolley bus and information drop along narrow streets of the old city center.

Suggestion of Real Losses

The newspaper said Donald, who was recruited while working at the Soviet Union's United Nations mission in New York, passed secret plans for defense against biological and chemical weapons to his American handlers. Other items included diplomatic codes, nuclear-weapons doctrine and civil defense preparations. . . .

Pravda suggested that Donald did considerable damage to Soviet defense and security.

"Having access to many state secrets, Donald was trading in everything the U.S. Intelligence services were interested in. With an excellent education and as a teacher in one of the academies, he was an expert in many questions," it said, without giving more details. . . .

According to the Pravda account, Donald more than once attracted the attention of K.G.B. counterintelligence agents, but managed to allay their suspicions with a cool head and meticulous precautions.

His love of danger and driving ambition fueled an astonishing career that ran from 1961 until his recent arrest and trial.

"I was accustomed to balancing on a knife edge and did not imagine any other life for myself," he was reported to have told his K.G.B. captors. He displayed no fear when arrested. . . .

Pravda said the spy's motives were not entirely clear, but it suggested that ideological disillusionment and personality—not money—prompted his betrayal.

Donald's exact position is not known, but there are suggestions he may have served as a diplomatic military counselor or even in the K.G.B. itself. (Reuters, 1990)

A Formidable Master Spy Ring

One of the most productive espionage operations prior to and during the early part of World War II was established in the Far East by the Soviet Union. A senior K.G.B. officer named Richard Sorge was the field officer in charge of the operation until it was uncovered by the Japanese.

Sorge was born in Russia in 1895, the son of a German father and a Russian mother. He was a charming and idealistic German national who later became a Soviet citizen. He turned to communism during World War I and shortly thereafter earned a Ph.D. in Political Science at Hamburg University. He was recruited for Soviet intelligence in 1925. By 1929 he had carried out several intelligence missions in Europe. He was next sent to Shanghai posing as a German journalist. In 1933 he returned to Moscow where he was praised and honored for his work in China. His next assignment would be Tokyo, his most important posting. On the way Sorge stopped off in Berlin to strengthen his credentials as a German journalist and to become a member of the Nazi Party.

Tension and conflict between Japan and the Soviet Union were of long standing. Until the mid-1930s the Kremlin considered Japan the greatest threat to the Soviet Union and placed a high priority on learning the military plans and intentions of the Japanese. Sorge arrived in Tokyo in 1933 to set up and operate his spy network. Another Soviet intelligence officer, also posing as a journalist, was sent to join him. Two others, a Japanese translator and a German radio operator, were also sent to work with Sorge in Tokyo. But the most significant member of this newly organized spy ring was Hotsumi Ozaki, who was recruited by Sorge earlier in Shanghi. He was a young Japanese idealist from a wealthy family with close relationships with the Japanese government. He would provide both access and the cover of legitimacy to reinforce Sorge's penetration skills.

It was not until 1936 that the Sorge ring was prepared to operate. By then Sorge himself was accepted as an unofficial adviser to the German embassy in Tokyo, with an office in the building and access to the files. He was also well established with the local Nazis and the resident representatives of the international press. He was perhaps the most knowledgeable Westerner in Japan at the time in terms of his understanding of Japanese politics and current affairs.

Meanwhile Ozaki had risen in the world. He became an established expert on Sino-Japanese relations, a high-level political analyst, a consultant to the Japanese Cabinet with an office in the offical residence of the Premier (Prince Konoye), and a member of his "kitchen cabinet," which advised the Premier on various national and international issues. In point of fact, by 1938 Sorge and Ozaki were not merely reporting state secrets to the K.G.B., they were helping to make these policy decisions themselves.

By this time the central mission of the Sorge Tokyo espionage ring was to warn of any pending attack on the Soviet Union by Japan. However, the Russo-Japanese Neutrality Treaty of 1941 lessened these Soviet concerns. Sorge now turned his intelligence gathering to determining the details of what appeared to be a forthcoming attack on Russia by Nazi Germany. After this actually occurred, Sorge's group again turned its attention to determining Japan's intentions toward Russia.

That Sorge was able to inform the K.G.B. early in October 1941 that there would be no attack on Russia by the Japanese until the spring of 1942 at the earliest enabled the Soviet Union to turn the full weight of the embattled Red Army to the defeat of the Germans.

This was the Sorge ring's greatest service to the Soviet Union, but it was accomplished in that grey area that divides the exercise of political influence from espionage. It can be argued that Sorge's message was merely a report on what he and Ozaki had already achieved— they had tilted the Japanese decision against an attack on Russia.

The ring had been uncovered almost entirely by accident. The Japanese police had been aware for some years of illegal radio transmissions originating somewhere in Tokyo. The navy and one or two government departments had complained about secrets leaking to the press. At the same time, Berlin had become concerned about Sorge's political past and a Gestapo officer going to Tokyo was instructed to report on Sorge. Against orders, this officer told the Japanese police of his mission, and they mistakenly got the impression that Sorge was under German surveillance because of security leaks from the embassy. They made a list of his associates and began to investigate them. Under torture, one of them confessed and named the other members of the ring. Sorge (49) and Ozaki (43) were hanged on November 7, 1944.[4]

NOTES

1. As used in this book, *espionage* refers to intelligence gathered by human agents. It does not refer to intelligence gathered by electronic means, satellite overflights, and various other devices for securing information.

2. In the United States, espionage is defined as violations of Title 18, Chapter 37 (Espionage and Censorship), Sections 792 through 799 of the U.S. Code. The titles of these sections and the penalties assigned to each are:

792—Harboring or concealing persons: fined not more than $10,000 or imprisoned not more than ten years, or both.

793—Gathering, transmitting, or losing defense information: fined not more than $10,000 or imprisoned not more than ten years, or both.

794—Gathering or delivering defense information to aid foreign government: punished by death or by imprisonment for any term of years or for life.

795—Photographing and sketching defense installations: fined not more than $1,000 or imprisoned not more than one year, or both.

796—Use of aircraft for photographing defense installations: fined not more than $1,000 or imprisoned not more than one year, or both.

797—Publication and sale of photographs of defense installations: fined not more than $1,000 or imprisoned not more than one year, or both.

798—Disclosure of classified information: fined not more than $10,000 or imprisoned not more than ten years, or both.

799—Violation of regulations of National Aeronautics and Space Administrations: fined not more than $5,000, or imprisoned not more than one year, or both.

From an examination of these section titles and from a reading of the statute itself, it becomes clear that violations of this chapter of the U.S. Code vary widely in terms of the actual behavior involved and in the severity of the penalties assigned. Only Section 794 (Gathering or delivering defense information to aid foreign government), which is the only section punishable by death or by imprisonment for any term of years or for life, involves behavior that conforms to the usual public image of what spies actually do.

3. By 1991, after the end of the Cold War, there was much debate among Washington leaders about the continued need for a Central Intelligence Agency, especially since there was no clear understanding of how the Agency would fit into the Bush Administration's "new world order." Spokesmen for the Administration maintained that the world was still a dangerous and unstable place, and that the CIA under new leadership would continue to monitor changes in the Soviet Union. The Agency would also emphasize tracking international drug smugglers and terrorists, monitoring world economic trends, protecting U.S. firms from industrial espionage, and developing intelligence about other threats to the U.S. economy and natural resources (Kurjian, 1991). Clearly, such a major shift in the mission of the CIA would alter considerably the mission of the American intelligence community in the coming decades. Such changes in the intelligence function would also complement some of the newer "low intensity warfare" overseas police missions of the U.S. military, as described in Chapter 1. The full consequences of the actual introduction in a major way of both the CIA and the military into law enforcement abroad against multinational crime cannot be precisely foreseen at this point. At a minimum such introduction would alter dramatically much of the meaning and practice of American criminal justice.

4. Adapted from Knightley (1986, pp. 185-192).

3

Drug-Trafficking and Arms-Trafficking

In considering drug-trafficking, it becomes clear that opium has been a commodity of world trade for more than 1,000 years. There is also a modern domestic counterpart to such trade in nations that consume illegal drugs. The purpose of this section is to present some of the apparent characteristics of multinational drug-trafficking systems for the purpose of suggesting some of what is known and what remains largely unknown about such systems.

As James Mills wrote in 1986, drug-trafficking has become an "underground empire" with a powerful, multinational political base. In summarizing his long narrative, it may be said that drug-trafficking appears to involve:

(1) innumerable actors organized into private and public economic networks or systems;

(2) a rather well defined division of labor on a multinational basis;

(3) a complex set of attitudes, values, and behavioral norms;

(4) production and distribution systems that are both domestic and multinational;

(5) avenues for "laundering" the flow of large cash profits;

(6) often a high level of violence;

(7) a complex set of relationships with governments of various nations that, in one way or another, find themselves related to, and sometimes profiting from, the traffic in drugs.

However, in considering such an empire, it may be in error to perceive it as under the control of an elite that rules from a central position of power. Rather, the empire may consist at any one time of a variety of groups, large or small, long-lasting or of short duration, to which individuals contribute their services and from which they gain their rewards. Further, it may be that those individuals holding superior positions in the various groups that constitute the illicit drug industry, or empire, are those who have the most control over three assets: (a) the ability to make "connections," that is, the ability to get things done, especially in a world of crooks with no police or courts to enforce contracts; (b) the control of swift and massive violence, and especially the reputation for controlling such violence without having to actually use it; and (c) the control over the corruption of law enforcement and various other officials (Moore, 1986; 1989).

History of Drug-Trafficking

The sophistication, complexity, and multinational political-economic organization of drug-trafficking are clearly borne out in history by the scope of the government-sanctioned opium trade with China that was forced on the people of that nation during the nineteenth century by European and American traders, especially the British. British trading entrepreneurs, backed by the British government and acting against the explicit legal prohibitions of the central Chinese government, bought opium in India that had been produced and auctioned by the British East India Company. To help pay the costs of governing India, they then smuggled large amounts of the drug through Canton and other Chinese ports to sell to China's addicts. Lacking a navy strong enough to challenge the British fleet, the Chinese government was never able to stop the traffic (Beeching, 1975; Chesneaux, Bastid, & Bergere, 1976; Fay, 1975).

In writing on the history of opium trading in Southeast Asia since about the eighth century, William J. Chambliss (1989) notes the early role of Turkish traders, followed during the sixteenth century by the Portuguese. By the time the French returned and succeeded in colonizing Indochina, starting in the mid-nineteenth century, the traffic in opium was a thriving business. The French joined with the traffickers and licensed opium dens throughout Indochina. With the profits, the French supported 50% of the cost of their colonial government in Indochina. When the Indochina War began with the Communists after World War II, the French used the opium profits to fight the insurgents, and cooperated with the hill tribes who controlled the opium to ensure their allegiance. After the French were defeated and withdrew from Vietnam, their place was taken by the United States, who inherited both the opium trade and the hill tribes. But the United States went further than the French. Using Air America, the CIA airline in Vietnam, bundles of illegal opium were regularly transported from airstrips in Laos, Cambodia, and Burma to the drug markets of Saigon and Hong Kong.

Opium had been known in China and in other parts of the Far East for 1,000 years by the time the British trade began with China. However, by the nineteenth century the opium traffic to China was dominated by the British; but the Americans were also involved. Through decades, however, mounting public criticism of U.S. opium-trafficking to China gradually brought about a reduction in participation. The U.S. opium trade to China dwindled to an insignificant level by 1880, when a Sino-American treaty prohibited such activity by Americans. Believing that it had cleared itself of all complicity in opium-trafficking to China, the United States government wrote it off as a Sino-British problem and officially stayed out of the matter for the remainder of the century. However, things began to change rapidly. Beginning in the twentieth century there was growing alarm that the misuse of narcotics was also a domestic problem for the United States and other Western powers. Involved were morphine, heroin, cocaine, and marijuana, with the principle sources of raw materials being the Far East, Turkey, Persia, Eastern Europe, Bolivia, and Peru (Taylor, 1969).

By 1990 the United States had developed a comparatively large addict population and a widespread fear of both drugs and addicts. In late-nineteenth and early-twentieth century America, addicts were identified with minorities: Chinese, Negroes, the "lower classes," and the "underworld." Much of the domestic fear fed the passage of the Harrison Act of 1914 (Musto, 1987, pp. 5-8, 65). This was the first legislation by the United States government that sought to control the

domestic traffic in opiates and cocaine. Since that time both the federal government and individual state governments have continued to enact and enforce various laws in a never-ending effort to control what has been defined by the public as the threat of domestic drug abuse and addiction. In the United States the drug problem, as David Musto (1987) had pointed out, has long been more of a political problem than a medical or legal one. In this country over the decades political reaction against drugs has been triggered by periods of mounting public agitation and concern. After a time the political response falters and declines as public pressure ebbs. In all the years since the growing fear of opiate and morphine addiction began in the late 1800s in the United States, the country has found no lasting solution to either its oscillating problem of drug abuse or the related problem of drug-trafficking. Despite high hopes, as first one is tried and then the other, both the medical and the law enforcement approaches have proved unsatisfactory, although even today each has its firm supporters.

International Efforts To Control Drugs

Equally true is that, since 1900, diplomatic and international efforts to control source country production and a wide range of trafficking interests have also not met with much success. The quest to control drug-trafficking is perhaps as much a problem for the United States today as it was for China back in 1840, if such historical comparisons make any sense. China of that period lacked the capacity to protect itself from a prohibited import, much the same as the United States and other Western nations today lack the capacity to stop the importation of illegal drugs.

The international movement to suppress the traffic in drugs, from the perspective of America's participation in it, started about 10 years before World War I and was concerned with drug traffic in the Far East. Early in the twentieth century China had undertaken a domestic anti-opium campaign, and Britain had virtually ended transporting opium from India to China. The Hague Opium Convention of 1912 provided for the participatory powers to help China and one another to solve their drug problems.

A second phase of the international movement covered the decade of the 1920s. During this period the United States tried to perfect its own domestic drug control legislation. Internationally the United States' efforts were complicated by the question of to what degree the United States, caught up in isolationism, should cooperate with the League of Nations. Furthermore, the United States felt that the League's drug policy reflected the self-interests of the opium bloc participant nations, which derived economic benefits from the drug traffic. Nevertheless, the United States made its position clear in international forums that the only acceptable purpose for the use of opium and other narcotics was strictly medical and scientific, and that the basic solution was to limit production of raw materials in source countries. But these principles were never ratified.

The third phase of the international movement to control drugs occurred during the 1930s. This time there was agreement through the League of Nations to limit manufacture of narcotic drugs to medical and scientific requirements. Less satisfactory gains were made to limit drug-trafficking itself. There was, however, a concerted effort at the source level to limit the production of raw materials. This period ended with the outbreak of World War II.

Throughout these three phases the self-righteous moral zeal that Americans brought to international conferences about drug control provided no answer to a fundamental political dilemma faced by many of the governments of other participants. These nations, unlike the United States, were characterized by very real and deep internal conflicts over drugs. Significant political, social, and economic groups within the drug-producing countries participating in the international discussions had strong vested interests in the continuation of drug-trafficking (Lamour & Lamberti, 1974; Taylor, 1969).

Today in many of the Third World source and transit countries that provide opium, heroin, and cocaine for Western industrialized consumer nations, the illegal drug industry is a most important source of foreign currency. The industry means jobs and investment capital in countries otherwise characterized by much poverty and unemployment.[1] In effect, the drug economy, although it has its disadvantages to be sure, appears to bring a measure of political stability to Third

World nations where ever-present rebel factions are waiting to exploit any weakness.

There seems to be a remarkable similarity between the conditions that prevail today and the importance of drugs in the economies of source and transit countries in earlier decades. Then as well as now, drugs declared illegal and banned on the initiatives of the West appear, upon closer scrutiny, to have been and continue to be important, even vital, contributors to the structural stability of source and transit nations.

Anslinger and Tompkins (1953) have also described the situation during the first half of the twentieth century, regarding multinational drug-trafficking and attempts at its control through the world-wide cooperation of diverse nations with varying, and sometimes conflicting, interests. By mid-century there was still no common accord to stop such trafficking, but by that time China was no longer targeted by the West as a market for its opium; instead, roles were reversed and Communist China was alleged in United Nations' debates to be one of the principal suppliers of opium and heroin to the United States and its Far Eastern Alliance. Clearly, the interests that nation-states had in drug-trafficking continued to depend on their relationships to the trade: Were they "sending" or "receiving" states? Were they politically aligned with one or the other?

Obviously, opium has been an important commodity in Far Eastern-European-American foreign relations for centuries. For Britain and France the opium trade was a significant way of funding their colonial enterprises: India in the case of Britain, and Indochina in the case of France. Once the United States became a major player during the 1960s in Vietnam, opium became an important basis for forging a link to indigenous tribes in the "Golden Triangle," thereby cementing their loyalty to the South Vietnamese-American partnership against the Communist Vietnamese. Since the withdrawal of the United States from South Vietnam in 1975, it appears that Laos, Myanmar (Burma), and Thailand have continued, and even increased, their production and trafficking in opium in a major way and are today defined as a serious threat to the drug control efforts of the West (Sciolino, 1990). Thus, the historical "opium trade" between Western nations and the Far

East continues. But this time the Western nations are much more on the receiving end of the opium-heroin pipeline. They are the consumer-nations while the Far Eastern source countries, their traffickers, and their bankers are the ones making the profits, expanding their economies, and advancing their political interests. The more dependent poor Far Eastern nations became upon the earnings of heroin sales to the West, the less responsive they are likely to become to Western requests for the reduction of their drug production. This may be particularly true if the West offers economic incentives that are far less than their drug earnings. Even if the incentives are substantial, the drug-producing nations may take them and continue to produce drugs at the same time.

The complex multinational character of drug-trafficking is also evidenced in more recent times by the descriptions of indigenous, government-linked, heroin-trafficking systems in Southeast Asia. Before the fall of South Vietnam, these systems moved raw opium and its derivatives out of the Golden Triangle to markets in Saigon, Europe, and the United States (McCoy, Read, & Adams, 1972). In the early 1970s, with the withdrawal of United States troops from South Vietnam, the Southeast Asian drug syndicates were awash in surplus heroin. With the American troop market dried up, these producers and traffickers turned to new outlets. One was Australia, which up to that time had relatively few addicts. By 1976 organized crime in Sydney had begun participating in an international network, which received heroin into Australia from the Golden Triangle for subsequent distribution locally and in the United States. During the same period the Sydney syndicate also began other facets of international expansion. This included investments in the Philippine prostitution industry and an alignment with the infamous Nugan Hand Bank of Sydney, which provided an international bridge between legitimate banks and organized crime, illegal money-laundering, arms-trading, and American intelligence operations. Currently, Australian syndicates, which began as parochial urban gangs in the 1920s, have expanded and taken on a multinational character similar to that of the American Mafia, the Chinese syndicates of Hong Kong and Southeast Asia, the French-Corsican syndicates, and others (McCoy, 1980; 1986).

Apparently much organized crime is now multinational, with drug-trafficking providing the foundations of its global power and enormous wealth.[2]

The Growing Interest of Political Science
In Drug-Trafficking

Political scientist Peter A. Lupsha (1981) has pointed out the various difficulties inherent in the adoption of the United States-sponsored drug-control policy by quite dissimilar drug-producing nations. One set of policy measures may well be moderately effective in Mexico, for example, with its strong and unified political culture, its stable control of the military, its effective government control of various geographic regions, and its containable corruption. However, just the opposite would apply in Colombia, with its fragmented political culture, its semi-independent military, its weak control of outlying regions, its rampant corruption, and its institutionalized violence—all of which add up to doubtful success for the drug control efforts of the United States within Colombia.

The increasing interest of political scientists in multinational drug-trafficking is illustrated by a special issue of the *Journal of Interamerican Studies and World Affairs* (Summer/Fall, 1988). This issue was devoted to 10 articles, mostly by political scientists, on the topic "Drug Trafficking in the Americas." In a foreword to the articles, Bruce Michael Bagley concluded:

(1) The articles agreed that to date the United States' War on Drugs had failed to diminish significantly the U.S.-Latin American drug trade. However, there was much less agreement about the impact of future United States policies.

(2) There was consensus that not enough is known about the many facets of the hemispheric drug trade. Considerable empirical research was needed to understand the economic, socio-cultural, political, and international dimensions of this multi-billion dollar growth industry.

(3) There was almost unanimous recognition of the need for conceptual work in the field to guide research and to interpret the findings. (Bagley, 1988)

Somewhat earlier *The Washington Quarterly* (Fall, 1985) devoted a section in one of its issues to the topic "High Policies: Drugs Across Borders." Written by political scientists, the four articles in this section give an overview of the evolution of the definition of the American drug problem from one of local street addiction to one of international politics; a description of the profound and most complex internal economic, political, and diverse ethnic/cultural characteristics of heroin and cocaine source areas in Southeast Asia and South America that make any real cooperation with United States overseas drug politics difficult; and the links between drugs and terrorism in various areas of the world.

History clearly demonstrates that multinational drug-trafficking is extremely difficult to control. Drug-trafficking systems, as with other aspects of world trade, appear to be sophisticated and complex organizations with close ties to various economic and political institutions on a national and multinational level. Multinational terrorism and espionage are also difficult to control for much the same reasons. They, too, are often carried on by complex multinational systems associated with military, intelligence, and diplomatic agencies, multinational corporations, and other powerful institutions of various nations or blocs of nations. It is this covert institutional linkage, which, offering various types of protection across national boundaries, makes the investigation, and certainly the prosecution, of participants in these multinational crime systems difficult and sometimes impossible.

Ethnographic Studies
of Drug-Trafficking

It is vital to understand that throughout history drug-trafficking has never been a benign economic activity played by gentlemen's rules. Always and everywhere drug-trafficking has been characterized by endemic violence. That many addicts commit crimes to feed their habits is not news. They shoplift, break and enter, mug, assault, rob banks, and sometimes even murder. This fact is well documented in the research literature on drug abuse and crime. Edward Preble and John J. Casey, Jr., in their classic article, "Taking Care of Business— The Heroin User's Life on the Street" (1969), amply described how the hustling, ever-active, ever-energetic, street addicts commit crime for profit to buy their heroin. In fact, in the late 1960s and early 1970s the federal government rapidly expanded methadone maintenance programs for heroin addicts as a major national strategy for reducing crime in the streets; the idea being that if heroin addicts could get free methadone, they would need to commit less crime in order to feed their habits.

Adler and Adler (1983) provided a very good first study of international marijuana and cocaine traffickers at the upper level of the industry in a large metropolitan area in southwestern California. They describe different routes into the upper world of drug-trafficking, oscillations in career patterns, and the difficulties of "final retirement" into legitimate work. The study traces the career processes involved in rising to the top as an upper-level dealer or smuggler in the "fast" and affluent lifestyle of international marijuana- and cocaine-trafficking.

Two years later Patricia Adler (1985) published a more extensive ethnographic study of marijuana- and cocaine-trafficking in the same California community. The dealers and smugglers she studied were mostly middle-class and white. They had no relationship to South American cocaine cartels, to Asian gangs, or to American organized crime. Essentially they were also nonviolent and depended on a personal reputation for fairness and honesty as a sanctioning mechanism. The chief attraction drug dealing had for them was that the profits enabled them to continue the hedonistic lifestyle to which they had grown accustomed.[3]

Drug-Trafficking Violence

What became news in recent years was that the "fast" life of the drug-trafficker in the United States frequently included wholesale violence committed to settle business disputes. Although references to predatory violence have often appeared in the research literature on drugs and crime, to a surprising degree such literature has not said much about the extremely violent crime and homicide committed for business reasons in drug-trafficking. It seems fair to state that many of the scholars interested in domestic drug abuse and crime either have been unaware or have chosen to ignore such drug-trafficking violence, as distinct from the more common predatory crimes of street addicts. Instead, they have often concentrated their research on crimes at the lowest level of drug distribution systems—the economic crimes of the domestic street addict. Few academic criminologists apparently have spent time studying business-oriented violence at the middle and upper levels of drug-trafficking. One exception to this can be found in *The War on Drugs,* by James A. Inciardi (1984), where he discusses the systemic violence in drug-trafficking in the United States and in Latin American cocaine-trafficking. Another is found in the theoretical work of Paul J. Goldstein (1982), who distinguishes between three models of violence associated with illegal drugs: psychopharmacological violence, in which specific individuals become violent after the ingestion of particular drugs; economically compulsive violence, when addicts rob and steal to pay for their habits; and systemic violence, which is intrinsic to much illegal drug-trafficking.

Although the violence and killings associated with drug-trafficking are currently newsworthy in the nation, experienced police officers, prosecutors, judges, and other criminal justice personnel have routinely dealt with such crimes for years. Perhaps one of the first empirical studies of drug-related homicides in a U.S. city was published by Heffernan, Martin, and Romano in 1982. This study was conducted in a police precinct in New York City that had a high number of homicides over several years. Some 50 of the homicides in the precinct during 1981 were examined, and 21, or 42%, were found to be drug-related. All 21 victims were shot to death with what, in the police idiom, are called "decent guns"—that is, weapons with heavy firepower. Upon investigation all appeared to have been killed because of drug-trafficking disputes.

The purpose here is to mark this violence as a topic of concern for the scientific community and, at the same time, to conceptualize and set forth in a preliminary fashion a perspective for addressing homicides in drug-trafficking systems above the level of predatory street-addict behavior. In keeping with the most recent trends away from absolutism in the study of deviance, an essential theoretical dimension for such field research is that it describe the particular deviant behavior being studied in terms of how those involved in such behavior describe what they are doing and why they are doing it. This point of view is well presented by Jack D. Douglas and Frances C. Wakster in their *The Sociology of Deviance: An Introduction* (1982). For example, do the killers who commit drug-trafficking homicides believe that their victims have violated rules essential to the proper conduct of the drug-trafficking business, and therefore morally deserve to be killed? Or are the value judgments made about the victims in these homicides much harsher—that is, is the norm-violating behavior of the victims defined as behavior that is absolutely evil? How widely are these definitions shared in the drug-trafficking community? Do answers to such questions help explain what often appears to outsiders to be the atrocious and even senseless nature of such killings, as for example when entire families, including children, are executed? A well-publicized case in New York City illustrates such a series of killings:

> Ten people were found shot to death in a Brooklyn apartment. Three were women, one was a teenage girl, and six were children. All had been shot in the head at close range. There was no sign of panic or struggle. The victims were all sitting up. "It looked like a wax museum." The bodies were found by Enrique Bermudez, the father of two of the children. At the time of the killings he was working as a taxi driver. It was reported that he had served 4 years in prison on narcotics charges, and he was also said to have recently purchased the small two-family house in which the killings took place with more than $50,000 in cash. Drug paraphernalia was found in the apartment where the bodies were discovered. Police suspect that the killings were motivated by revenge and were linked to Colombian narcotics dealers.[4]

In terms of the violent crime endemic to these drug-trafficking systems, several points need to be emphasized:

(1) Each of these drug distribution systems is entirely illegal in the United States;

(2) each has its own supply and distribution system, either centralized or dispersed, as the case may be;

(3) each has its own conduct norms, "contracts," and rules of procedure, which are typically unwritten but clearly understood by participants as cultural specifications and imperatives;

(4) none of the contracts, social norms, agreements, or competitive practices can be regulated by the courts or regulatory agencies, as is the case with legitimate businesses; and

(5) many of the systems are functionally dependent on violence as a sanctioning mechanism for the violation of norms, contracts, and agreements, and for the reduction of competition.

Thus, the use of threat, intimidation, assault, and homicide is functionally essential for the maintenance and expansion of profit-taking in many heroin-, cocaine-, and marijuana-trafficking systems. It is not only the low-level violence of the street addict robbing to feed his habit that is of primary significance in understanding the violence of drug-trafficking. Rather, it is also the wholesale use of assault and homicide at middle and upper levels of these systems that is of central importance for a public understanding of their pernicious and malignant domestic destructiveness. Thus, from top to bottom many drug distribution systems appear to be built, sustained, and maintained by violence or the threat of violence. This violence is of such magnitude, that it contributes substantially to the rising rate of violent crimes in major U.S. urban areas—for example, drug-related homicides now constitute a large proportion of all homicides in many cities. Finally, it does not appear that the violence and homicide endemic to drug-trafficking systems are being met effectively by present law enforcement intervention strategies. To a surprising degree, for example, in contrast with other homicides, those in drug-trafficking systems do not appear to be easily solved and the perpetrators arrested, indicted, convicted, and sentenced. As in long-standing forms of organized crime homicides, drug-trafficking homicides are difficult to solve. Frequently, the killers are not even identified.

When attention is shifted from drug-related systemic violence in U.S. cities to large-scale drug-related violence in illegal drug source countries such as Colombia and Peru, it may be useful to use a new term to identify such behavior: drug-related mega-violence. Such mega-violence usually appears to be well organized and sustained. It is usually directed at government officials, newspaper editors, and

other influential citizens. At an extreme it may tax the capacity of
the government to maintain itself. Finally, it may arise out of a pragmatic, nonideological union of drug-trafficking cartels and indigenous
guerrilla groups, who, it would appear, cooperate to strike violently at
establishment targets. Such violence has been called narco-terrorism.[5]
In both qualitative and quantitative terms, such mega-violence is significantly different from both the violence of the predatory street
addict and the systemic violence of domestic drug-traffickers in U.S.
cities. In addition to being systemic, large-scale, and sustained, it is also
politically motivated—that is, aimed at achieving some order of governmental change—which does not appear to be the case with other
drug-related violence. The kinds of extremely complicated pragmatic
scenarios that the different parties involved in narco-terrorism may
have in fact worked out with one another may not be readily apparent. (A further discussion of the interrelationship between terrorism
and drug-trafficking is found in Chapter 4.)

CASE MATERIAL ABOUT DRUG-TRAFFICKING

The Illegal Drug Industry
in the United States

A report by the U.S. Attorney General to the President in August
1989 describes what may be called multinational, as well as domestic, organizations marketing illegal drugs in the United States. The
principal multinational organizations are:

Colombian Drug Cartels. These large, vertically integrated *cocaine-
trafficking* groups are involved in production, supply, and sale of the
illicit product, aided by accountants, chemists, lawyers, paid politicians, and corrupt customs officials. Bribery and assassination are
frequently used. The cartels operate not only in Colombia, where
they are becoming more accepted, and in the United States, but also
in other parts of the world. The cartels are now major landowners in
Colombia, with extensive real estate interests in the city of Medellín,
one of their centers of influence. More than just a criminal enterprise
in their native land, the cartels have become "a veritable state within

a state." Elsewhere, besides their widespread trafficking activities throughout the United States, they are active in the Bahamas, the Turks and Caicos Islands, Panama, and Cuba.

La Cosa Nostra and the Sicilian Mafia. The former was founded in the United States during the 1930s by Italian immigrant criminals. The Sicilian Mafia began as a major southern Italy secret society, but has become active in organized crime in the United States, independent of La Cosa Nostra. However, both groups associate and criminally interact in a number of areas of mutual interest, including both *heroin-* and *cocaine-trafficking.* Heroin is introduced to the United States market from Southwest and Southeast Asia, and cocaine from South America. Both organizations are involved in many aspects of organized crime in addition to drug-trafficking. The style of both is to cooperate and coexist with Asian, Colombian, and other drug-trafficking groups doing business in the United States.

Asian Organized Crime Groups. Asian gangs, primarily of Chinese origin, have been a major force in the U.S. illicit drug market since about 1985. Chinese organized crime leaders in this country have used their ties to Asian overseas criminal organizations to import illegal goods, including *heroin,* to the United States. Other Chinese crime groups active in the United States are the Triads, although Hong Kong serves as their primary base of operations. The Triads originated in China during the seventeenth century to oppose the rule of the Manchu dynasty. Today they are involved in a number of rackets worldwide, of which drug-trafficking is but one part. Chinese Tongs, which began as legitimate mutual aid societies for Chinese immigrants in the United States, have usually remained legitimate. Some Tongs have become affiliated with Chinese street gangs. (Asian organized crime groups are described in greater detail in Chapter 4).

Jamaican Posses. Approximately 40 vertically integrated Jamaican organized crime gangs operate in the United States, Canada, Great Britain, and the Caribbean. These gangs generally grew out of specific geographic and political affiliations in Jamaica, but have long since become exclusively profit-oriented drug-trafficking organizations.

Marijuana and *cocaine* are the principal illegal drugs supplied by the Jamaican Posses that have emerged as major drug-traffickers since the mid-1980s. The posses are highly mobile and violent toward one another and toward law-enforcement officers. The posses have developed close working relationships with Colombians, Cubans, West Coast street gangs, and other major players in drug-trafficking.

Other groups, such as outlaw motorcycle gangs and California street gangs, have specialized in domestic drug-trafficking in various parts of the country. Still other domestic groups have focused on drug-dealing in particular urban areas. Not all domestic trafficking groups operate in poor urban areas. Some are run by middle-aged whites living in affluent suburbs, still others are operated by upper middle-class whites and Hispanics. In parts of the rural Southeast, people, often families, who once produced moonshine or engaged in local crime now grow marijuana or traffic in cocaine.

Many foreign nationals in addition to those already cited also engage in organized drug-trafficking, according to the Attorney General, including Mexican nationals operating especially in the Southwest and Far West, Dominican Republic nationals, migratory Haitian workers, Nigerian smugglers, Cuban nationals, and others. These groups appear to be highly mobile and less well organized than the principal trafficking organizations, and generally operate locally or regionally; some have been very violent in protecting their interests.

As the nation enters the 1990s, the impact of the world's illegal drug trade appears to be escalating. In 1990 the illegal drug trade was estimated to be worth $500 billion a year. This was larger than the world trade in oil and second only to the arms trade (Lewis, 1990). A U.S. State Department report in early 1990 noted that the global production of opium poppies, coca, marijuana, and hashish soared during 1989. This occurred despite the highly publicized effort of the United States to curtail drug supply and demand. Worldwide drug abuse has increased as new markets have been opened to take up the available supply (Sciolino, 1990).

Profits from such trafficking are enormous. Domestic violence in the United States and mega-violence in Third World countries that supply consuming nations with illegal drugs have become matters of worldwide concern. Policies both at home and abroad to control drug-trafficking have generally had little success. Illegal drugs continue to arrive in increasing volume in the United States. The need for basic research to increase an understanding of the phenomenon is pressing. *The National Drug Control Strategy* (The White House, 1989) calls for "a much better understanding of the structure and infrastructure of trafficking organizations and allied enterprises." To do this successfully, the strategy maintains, appropriate federal, state, and local information sources must be utilized; overseas collection of information through the Drug Enforcement Administration, the Central Intelligence Agency, the Department of Defense, and the State Department will have to be incorporated; major drug production and traficking organizations that are complex, highly organized, and efficient as international businesses will have to be analyzed; a complete and accurate picture of entire drug-trafficking enterprises will have to be created to strike at the heart of drug-trafficking rather than at its periphery. This is the research agenda set down by the *National Drug Control Strategy*. It is a tough assignment.

ARMS-TRAFFICKING

Often related to national intelligence agencies, terrorist groups, and drug-traffickers, the world's arms suppliers, who are either nation-states or private entrepreneurs, meet their clients' needs for weapons. On the one hand, such suppliers sell or transfer arms to allied governments in full accord with the policies of the nations involved; on the other, such organizations sometimes supply arms to clients in violation of the policies and the laws of at least some of the nations involved. In the latter cases, the label "arms-trafficker" is usually applied, signifying the illegal nature of the trade. In this book the object of attention is illegal arms-trafficking, not legal arms trading or arms transfers from one nation to another, although all three may be judged morally reprehensible by some. Whether the sale or transfer of arms is legal or illegal, considerable organization appears essential; in fact, illegal arms-trading may well require more sophisticated organizational methods than those essential to the legal sales or transfer of arms. In the more complicated aspects of this illegal traffic, the trade craft of the intelligence community often appears to be utilized to conceal what is actually taking place. Such trafficking is scarcely the work of one or two individuals in government or the private sector. In varying degrees, it requires the clandestine cooperation of various organizations, both public and private, on an international level. The labyrinth of intrigue and organization involved in multinational arms-trading, both legal and illegal, by a rogue CIA agent is well described in *Manhunt* by Peter Maas (1986).

Trading in arms, sometimes legal and sometimes illegal, dates back to the time of the Crusades, but the trade did not become global until the modern armaments industry began in the mid-nineteenth century, soon after the start of the Industrial Revolution (Sampson, 1977, p. 21). Today arms sales or transfers have become a crucial dimension of international affairs. Since the late 1960s, arms sales or transfers to the developing nations of the world have undergone an especially dramatic expansion, with the largest share since the later 1970s going to the Persian Gulf and the Middle East, and the next-largest to Africa and Latin America. Such imports from the industrialized world are a major factor in the emergence of Third World regional powers. Thus, such purchases do not simply involve economics; they also have crucial political significance (Pierre, 1982). Therefore, it is most important that any effort to understand multinational arms-trafficking focuses sharply on the political aspects of the trade.

It is clear that military assistance programs to implement arms transfers from one nation to another may do much to enhance the influence of the donor nation with its client state. When sizable transfers are taking place, the exchange of military personnel for training also often occurs. Replacement and spare parts dependencies develop. Other relationships also develop. It is interesting in this regard that China has emerged as one of the "big four" nations as a supplier of arms to developing countries (Blechman & Kaplan, 1978, pp. 10-11). Thus, in 1988 a Congressional Research Service study reported that mainland China had emerged as one of the leading suppliers of arms to developing nations. China ranked behind the Soviet Union, the United States, and France in terms of arms sales. Overall, the report said, the value of arms sales with developing nations in 1987 was $30 billion, with the United States agreeing to sell $5.6 billion worth of arms to such nations that year (Cushman, 1988).

An interesting aspect of China's increased overseas trade in weapons is found in a 1989 special report of the U.S. Drug Enforcement Administration about the illegal trafficking in Chinese-made AK-47 assault rifles from their points of legal importation to private gun dealers in California to their illegal smuggling to drug-traffickers in Mexico and Colombia. The report notes that drugs were sometimes used instead of cash to pay the smugglers for the weapons. This case illustrates one type of cooperative relationship between private arms-traffickers and drug-traffickers. The former supply the latter with illegal arms; the latter pay for the arms with illegal drugs, and presumably the arms-traffickers then sell the drugs for cash with a suitable markup in the value of the drugs involved.

The illegal trade in American-made small arms from the United States to Latin America is a well established pattern. The United States is one of the major manufacturers of firearms in the world. By contrast most countries in Latin America, like Mexico and Costa Rica, have stringent gun laws prohibiting citizens from acquiring or possessing guns. Further, in Mexico, for example, no gun factories are operating. With demand for guns increasing in Latin America, increased trafficking occurs from the United States to meet this market need (Gerth & Brinkley, 1985). Thus, in the starkest terms, a deadly two-way illegal trade pattern appears to exist between Latin America and the United States: We are rich in the production of small arms, many of which are sold illegally to meet the market demands of Latin America. In turn, Latin America is rich in cocaine, which is sold illegally to meet the market demands of the United States.

Much arms-trafficking appears to be entirely economic behavior. No political motivation seems evident. However, quite clearly arms-trafficking by private groups may also be highly political in its motivation. Such was the case with the so-called Harrison-Carter network of American Irish Republican Army sympathizers, who, starting in the 1950s, smuggled weapons to Northern Ireland for some 20 years.

The two leaders were motivated by a common goal, the establishment of a United Irish Republic. There was not hint of economic profit (Holland, 1987).

Domestic Arms-Trafficking

Arms-trafficking can also be small-scale and domestic instead of multinational. For example, street gangs in northern cities in the United States may send members to buy guns in southern states that have less strict gun control laws. The guns are then smuggled in small lots across state lines for use by the northern gangs.

It is significant to note that, in an analysis of illegal firearms recovered in New York City during 1981, 1982, and through August 1983, certain states were identified as the primary sources of the flow of illegal firearms into the New York City area. The principal source states were Florida, Virginia, South Carolina, Texas, and Georgia, where there exist either minimal or no licensing requirements with respect to handguns. A majority of the recovered firearms less than one year old surfaced in selected police precincts in New York City. New York City has a strict law regulating the purchase of legal handguns. This, the study concludes, encourages the flow of illegal guns from the five Southern states cited to the New York City area (U.S. Bureau of Alcohol, Tobacco & Firearms, n.d.).

A spontaneous and unorganized domestic black market in infantry light arms sprang up in Panama, a nation of 2.4 million people, after General Manuel Antonio Noriega was ousted by the U.S. Army in December 1989. The anarchy that followed the invasion by United States forces convinced many middle-class Panamanians to buy black-market arms left by Noriega's forces after their defeat.

Soon after the invasion the United States inaugurated a program to buy arms from citizens for cash, with no questions asked. Some 20 days after the invasion the U.S. Army had paid $798,100 for 8,769 weapons, which, when added to the weapons seized from Noriega's strongholds, totaled 76,553 weapons brought under Army control. Yet the supply of weapons still available in Panama remained very large, it would seem. On the black market, AK-47 and M-16 automatic rifles were selling to eager citizens for $350 and $250, respectively. This was two to three times what the U.S. Army was paying.[6]

Arms Entrepreneurs

As the following case illustrates, it should not be concluded from the above examples that private arms traders are necessarily small-timers. The subject of the case is reported elsewhere (Kwitny, 1987, p. 121) to have been a former CIA career officer whom the CIA set up in the private arms business.

> In the late 1970s an arms trader by the name of Sam Cummings was described as the most successful of small-arms dealers. He was the chairman and principal shareholder in the Interarms Company situated in Manchester, in Great Britain. His six-story warehouse contained no fewer than 300,000 weapons waiting to be shipped to whatever government or company would pay for them. At that time he had been in the small-arms trade for over twenty-five years. Formerly he had been employed by the CIA to help identify captured weapons in the Korean war; later he worked for a California arms company which made handsome profits from selling surplus arms to the American public and to the CIA for its clandestine operations. Still later he established his own private arsenal in Alexandria, Virginia, and sold guns to the regimes of Latin America, buying up huge quantities of surplus small arms from Europe and the Middle East. He didn't deal in small quantities even during these early days: 2,000 small arms bought from the Israelis after the Suez war of 1956; a million Lee-Enfield rifles bought from the British government in the late 1950s. By this time Cummings was established as the world's leading private arms dealer, although he claims never to have exceeded an annual turnover of $100 million. It is difficult to tell from conversations with Cummings whether or not his arms deals have always been legal. For him the eleventh commandment is: "Thou shalt not be found out." (Sampson, 1977, pp. 24-32)

Perhaps the best description of the world of private arms dealers is found in George Thayer's *The War Business: The International Trade in Armaments* (1969). Here he describes three types of private dealers: the big-time dealers, such as Cummings described above; the "munitions manipulators," who operate small organizations and who are versatile and can work their way around government policies and embargoes and get arms delivered to clients when big-time dealers back away to avoid risks and negative consequences; and the gun-runners, who specialize in the outright illegal introduction of arms into a country or region. Some gunrunners are independent operators, while others are government intelligence agencies, such as the Central Intelligence Agency, the secret intelligence agencies of other democracies, and the intelligence agencies of various Communist governments. In still other countries, such as Algeria and Egypt, special government agencies perform such tasks.

In 1988 Michael T. Klare published an article, titled "Secret Operatives, Clandestine Trades: The Thriving Black Market for Weapons," in which he summarized much of what was known about illegal arms-trafficking. Most significant perhaps, for the purposes of this book, is his conclusion that despite the obvious significance of illegal arms transactions, little information or analysis about such crime exists in the academic or professional literature. Klare maintains that the black-market traffic in arms accounts for as much as one-third of the dollar value of all international arms transfers. Surprisingly perhaps, the author concludes that "the interdiction of illicit arms exports from the United States is given a relatively low priority by the federal bureaucracy, producing little resistance to such transfers. Poor management of the Pentagon's arms stockpiles compounds the problem." The author goes on to state: "Furthermore, there seems to be no significant effort by any party to stem the flow of illegal arms to terrorists, insurgents, nations at war, or pariah states like Libya and South Africa."

Arms Transfers by Governments

Industrial nation-states have long engaged in legal arms transfers to their allies and client states. Such nation-states have also engaged in a variety of covert actions with respect to other countries—covert actions that have ranged from propaganda campaigns to paramilitary operations against other governments (Treverton, 1987).

Perhaps the most publicized unsuccessful covert action by the United States in recent years was the Iran-Contra Affair (Inouye & Hamilton, 1988). The exposure of this action started simply:

At about noon on Sunday October 5, 1986, an old C-123 plane being operated by an American air carrier "front" was flying ammunition and supplies into Nicaragua to support the Contra rebels against the Nicaraguan government which was opposed by the United States. The plane was shot down by a ground-to-air missile and crashed into the Nicaraguan countryside. An American ex-Marine who was part of the crew of the aircraft parachuted to safety. He was apprehended, brought to trial by the Nicaraguan government, found guilty and sentenced to 30 years in prison. However, he was soon pardoned and released. The shoot-down and trial, however, were given wide publicity. (Gutman, 1988, pp. 337-338)

Thus began the unraveling of President Ronald Reagan's National Security Council's initiative to free the hostages in Iran by selling weapons to that country, while at the same time continuing to supply the Contra forces attacking Nicaragua when the supply of weapons to such forces had been prohibited by Congress. Various official reports, congressional hearings, the appointment of a special prosecutor, indictments, and trials in federal court followed in the ensuing 3 or more years. It is significant to note here, perhaps, that none of the principals in the Iran-Contra Affair was ever found guilty of any crimes for the sale of weapons to Iran, the diversion of the profits from that into the private sector, and the resupply of the Contras with weapons when such had been prohibited by Congress. The only person convicted of supplying weapons was the ex-Marine crew member of the C-123 cargo plane shot down in October 1986, and he was convicted in a Nicaraguan court.

CASE MATERIAL ABOUT ARMS-TRAFFICKING

Chinese Arms Smuggling:
An Aspect of International Trade

The following news item describes a multinational arms-trafficking network, which smuggled Chinese-made AK-47 assault rifles into the United States to American gun dealers. Two Chinese trading companies that are part of the Chinese government are identified as having been involved in the network. Both companies have links to the

Chinese army and sell surplus military equipment abroad to raise hard currency.

LOS ANGELES, May 8—Agents of the Bureau of Alcohol, Tobacco and Firearms have found duplicated serial numbers, irregular markings and other signs of possible wide-spread smuggling of Chinese-made AK-47 assault rifles into the United States, according to sources close to the investigation.

In one case, the same serial number appeared on six weapons and sources said that suggests that tens of thousands of the military-style semiautomatics may have entered the country undetected in the last three years. Many weapons also have had no required place of origin or import markings, making them more difficult to trace if used in crimes. The initial investigation and the acknowledged inability of Customs agents to check most shipping containers for contraband reveal difficulties awaiting any attempt by the Bush administration to make permanent its temporary ban on imports of semiautomatic assault weapons. According to bureau estimates, as many as 80,000 AK-47s may have entered the country legally since 1986. The sudden import explosion and the slaying with an AK-47 of five school children in California in January led to the temporary ban.

But federal investigators are examining the possibility that many more AK-47s have reached U.S. buyers undetected in violation of import, firearms and tax laws. One dealer who has cooperated with bureau agents said he was told that the number of smuggled weapons could be as high as 500,000.

Customs officials, just beginning to look for illegal gun imports after years of focusing on narcotics, noted that, at the port of Los Angeles, only 1,500, or 2 percent, of 75,000 monthly container shipments can be examined completely. "You just get beat by the volume," said Ian Sang, a veteran chief inspector.

Containers of heavy ammunition boxes or unrelated cargo provide useful cover for arms smugglers. "If you want to hide anything, you hide it in the nose of the container," said Sang, referring to the deepest part of a 20- or 40-foot-long metal shipping container.

John Huey, a gun salesman in Los Angeles, said he first saw improperly marked AK-47s in late 1987 when customers brought in weapons they had purchased elsewhere for an unusually low price of $258 each. Stamped on each weapon was a serial number and a notation "56S" but no federally required identification marks showing model, caliber, manufacturer, importer, country of origin and importer's city and state. Huey said the weapons' quality and style indicated that they were supplied by Poly Technologies (Polytech), one of two principal Chinese trading companies handling AK-47s and similar firearms.

"I'd never seen AKs or any foreign gun that didn't have a point of origin," Huey said. "I just didn't know how they could do that unless they were smuggled."

Another dealer, who asked not to be identified, said he found weapons apparently supplied by China North Industries Corp. (Norinco), the other principal Chinese supplier, in another city in the Southwest months later with the same missing markings. He said he also purchased similarly unmarked Polytech rifles through a California importer. . . .

Sang, who has worked for Customs for 20 years, said he anticipates increased smuggling if the import ban is made permanent. "Our main focus has been narcotics," he said. Sang added that those who have profited from smuggling cocaine and heroin, "I don't think are going to be adverse to bringing weapons in". [7]

Across The Mexican Border:
A Guns for Drugs Underground Market

The U.S. Attorney for the Western District of Texas reports, as described in the next news story, that thousands of assault weapons are regularly smuggled each year across the Texas border to arm Mexican drug dealers. The yearly value of the weapons is reported to be about $250 million. One popular weapon involved is a lighter Chinese version of the Soviet-made AK-47. The U.S. Attorney also reports that the smuggled weapons are often exchanged for drugs, not cash. This smuggling of weapons into Mexico has been going on regularly at least since 1986, frequently with the help of Spanish-speaking United States federal employees who are often related to the drug-traffickers.

About $250 million in assault weapons is smuggled across the border to Mexican drug dealers each year, the U.S. Attorney for the Western District of Texas has told President Bush.

The report also indicates that some federal employees working along the border are related to the drug runners and even help them move their illicit goods into the United States.

Those drug traffickers are heavily armed with the latest in firearm technology, the report states.

Such state-of-the-art weaponry includes semiautomatic rifles and pistols converted to fully automatic, and high-powered rifles are among the illegal caches crossing the border each year, the report indicates.

One popular assault weapon found across the board is the AKS—a lighter Chinese version of the famed Soviet-made AK-47.

Agents with the U.S. Bureau of Alcohol, Tobacco and Firearms in the Rio Grande Valley have either traced or identified 7,500 legally sold para-military weapons that were smuggled into Mexico in one month alone last year, the report states.

Phil Chojnacki, the bureau's special agent-in-charge in Houston, cited another case in Laredo in which 7,300 firearms were known to have moved across the border illegally in 1986. Many times those weapons are traded for drugs, as shown in the case earlier this month in which a man pleaded guilty in a San Antonio federal court to plotting a guns-for-drugs deal.

The report also states that agents have uncovered evidence that federal employees working along with others have profited from smuggling cocaine and heroin.

According to one dealer, investigators want to know if importers of improperly marked weapons escaped paying excise taxes. "They're trying to make a three- or four-pronged case: Tax evasion, smuggling, antitrust and RICO," the dealer said, referring to the Racketeer Influenced and Corrupt Organizations Act.

The antitrust case, the dealer said, would attempt to prove that Chinese companies are conspiring to fix AK-47 prices. Although some China experts have blamed the AK-47 import surge on competition between Chinese companies for the lucrative U.S. market, the dealer said investigators are exploring the possibility that "Norinco and Polytech are really under the same entity. They are Chinese government organizations, and therefore they've come with the same product, with a high price and a low price, and saturated the market."

Dick Gillespie, vice-president of the U.S. China Business Council based in Washington, said both companies had links to the Chinese army and sold military equipment abroad to raise hard currency for purchase of foreign technology.

Gillespie said the companies' activities reflected "a lot of pressure on the defense industry" to find foreign buyers for equipment no longer needed by the Chinese military.

"It's hard to find Spanish speakers willing to take those jobs on the border, and often they end up going to people who have lived there in those towns all their lives," the U.S. Attorney said.

The cultural makeup of the Texas border is such that often federal workers are related to the drug traffickers in Mexico. [8]

* * *

The motivations of individual participants in the different case materials presented in Chapter 2 and in the present chapter appear to vary widely. Some appear to be motivated by hate or revenge, some by their national political interests, and some by economic gain. Often motivation is not clear and at best can only be inferred.

In the examples presented ethnic or religious group identification is sometimes shared by the groups described, and sometimes family memberships are also involved. It is possible that, in the United States and in various other countries where multinational systemic crime is well established, ethnic or religious identification plays a significant role in structuring the membership of existing and emergent criminal organizations. The process of ethnic succession is clearly evident in terms of changes that have been and continue to be occurring in domestic organized crime in the United States. The suggestion here is that ethnic or religious identifications may also be significant as organizing elements in the development of a number of multinational crime networks in various parts of the world. Examples are numerous: the Colombian cocaine cartels, Hong Kong-based Chinese Triad heroin smugglers, Shiite Muslim Party of God terrorists in Lebanon, and so on. Many different variables are likely to be at work in accounting for the cultural homogeneity of the membership of the various crime networks. A shared sense of oppression through the generations, the loyalty and trust of kinship, a group's proximity to drug-producing source areas, a centuries-old tradition of ethnic involvement in rigidly organized criminal groups, and many other possibilities exist. Such identifications may serve a powerful unifying function in such organizations, insulating them from outside intervention by law enforcement and conflicting criminal groups, while at the same time insuring in-group members of group support, which appears to be especially important for a sense of personal security in strange and even hostile environments.

NOTES

1. For a discussion of the cocaine trade and South American economies, see Lee (1989, pp. 35-50).

2. For a description of the Sicilian Mafia's rapid rise to global power and wealth on the basis of its drug-trafficking, see Sterling (1990).

3. For a description of a highly profitable and efficient white, middle-class, non-violent, drug-trafficking and money-laundering ring operating out of Scranton, Pennsylvania, during the early 1980s, see Rice (1989). This ring was composed of a nucleus of pilots and mechanics, which ran a criminal enterprise engaged in the sale and modification of light aircraft ideally suited for smuggling cocaine from Colombia to the United States. But the millions of dollars earned by the pilots was chiefly from flying such aircraft from South America, delivering cocaine for the Medellín cartel.

4. Adapted from McFadden (1984) and Shenon (1984).

5 For a discussion of narco-terrorism from a global perspective, see Long (1990); Lupsha (1988).

6. Adapted from Marquis (1990).

7. Reprinted from the U.S. Bureau of Alcohol, Tobacco & Firearms (June 1, 1989).

8. Adapted from the U.S. Bureau of Alcohol, Tobacco & Firearms (September 1, 1989).

4

Three Pertinent Observations

This chapter considers three observations pertinent to the study of multinational systemic crime. The first describes the interrelationships that may occur between types of multinational crime, then describes the linkage between one type of such crime, drug-trafficking, and domestic organized crime in the United States. The second examines the influence of ideology on criminological theory; the relationship of theory to current U. S. domestic crime control policy; and the impact of geopolitical restraints on the application of such policy overseas. The third presents a discussion of the constraints posed by possible "national security" declarations prohibiting access to data for research on multinational systemic crime.

MULTINATIONAL SYSTEMIC CRIME: INTERRELATIONSHIPS, DRUG-TRAFFICKING LINKS TO ORGANIZED CRIME

The four multinational crime systems considered in this book should be perceived as four systems that, in a variety of ways, may be interrelated. Since these are clandestine systems that frequently operate under the protection of one or more governments, firm evidence supporting their activities and their interrelatedness is not easily uncovered. Despite this difficulty it seems appropriate to assume tentatively, on the basis of existing evidence, that these systems are sometimes interrelated. Thus, terrorists may sometimes join others in the traffic in drugs; drug-lords may sometimes commit acts of terrorism against one another in coalition with others, or use violence against governments; intelligence agencies may sometimes aid in the traffic in arms, and so on through varying combinations.

Given this background, the study of multinational crime might endeavor to establish in far greater detail the actual patterns of interrelationship between different types of such crime, and various alliances of the groups involved in them. What follows is a summary of some of the literature that illustrates the complexity of these relationships and alliances.

Richard Craig (1987) has called attention to some of these combinations, which he found in South America during the middle 1980s. In Bolivia, for example, he described the drug-processing zones as characterized by endemic corruption and violence, with an influx of external traffickers and a widespread illicit commerce in automatic weapons. In Colombia, where the narcotics industry employed perhaps 500,000, he found that the cocaine drug-lords and guerrillas were "kindred spirits." Both were terrorists because of their tactics and violence. Acting alone or together, they challenged the very existence of government.

A United Nations report released in 1987 closely linked illegal drug production and trafficking with the illegal arms trade and international terrorism and subversion. The report also drew attention to the vast sums of money generated by illegal drug sales, which are laundered through legitimate enterprises, worldwide. The report further stated that wherever illicit drug cultivation, production, and trafficking occur, drug abuse by the local population almost inevitably ensues. This has happened in Africa, for example, in India, in Pakistan, and in such places as Afghanistan, Iran, Burma, and Thailand (Sciolino, 1987).

A complex secret relationship between the U. S. government, the transportation of illegal arms, and drug-trafficking was alleged by Leslie Cockburn in her 1987 book, *Out of Control: The Story of the Reagan Administrations' Secret War in Nicaragua, the Illegal Arms Pipeline, and the Contra Drug Connection*. Essentially she argu-ed that airplanes and pilots, operating under contract for the resupply of the Contras, repeatedly flew arms from Florida to clandestine airstrips in Costa Rica, El Salvador, and elsewhere in Central America. These airplanes then returned with loads of marijuana and cocaine. At the same time, the

Drug Enforcement Administration, the Central Intelligence Agency, the U.S. Attorney in Miami, and other federal agencies were, Cockburn reports, protecting this Contra shuttle service by discrediting the informants who reported it, by stating flatly that Contra drug-trafficking did not exist, and by stating that individual contract pilots might be transporting drugs by taking advantage of the inspection-avoidance system on such flights that had been set up the Central Intelligence Agency with the U.S. Customs Service. Such pilots acting as "freelancers" might be transporting some illegal drugs, said the Customs Service, but that was different from having the operation approved by the government.

Regardless of whether it was actually approved by the government, the Nicaraguan Contra supply system may well have served as a source for illegal drugs entering the United States from Central America. This appears especially likely since many of the pilots hired, according to Cockburn, had been successful drug-traffickers before signing on for the Contra resupply flights.

Ben Bradlee, Jr. (1988), in his biography of former Marine Lieutenant Colonel Oliver North, who played a central role in the Iran-Contra Affair, cites further evidence of Contra involvement in drug-trafficking. In his chapter titled "Guns Down, Drugs Up," Bradlee wrote:

> With the need for funds seemingly always desperate, some leading Contra supporters used profits from the sale of drugs to buy weapons and supplies for the resistance, according to those involved, and to testimony before the Senate Subcommittee on Terrorism, Narcotics and International Operations. "I'm not proud of it, but we didn't have any choice," one Contra leader, Octaviano Cesar, told the subcommittee in April of 1988. "I mean, the U.S. Congress didn't give us any choice" when it adopted the Boland Amendment in late 1984 cutting off further funding. Cesar said he himself was not a dealer, but he had been aware that some of the Contras' support was coming from drug dealers.
>
> One of those dealers, convicted drug smuggler George Morales, a Colombian serving a sixteen-year federal-prison sentence, told the committee that several U.S. government agencies, including the CIA, were aware that he was channeling "millions of dollars" in drug profits to the Contras and approved of it.

In January 1990, soon after General Manuel Antonio Noriega was seized in Panama, the press carried reports of his varying involvements in elaborate eavesdropping and other intelligence operations in Panama, his close links to Cuban intelligence, and his employment as a valuable intelligence source for the U.S. Army. In 1977 the Carter Administration, in order to win ratification of the Panama Canal Treaty, played down General Noriega's drug activities and his role in espionage against the United States. American intelligence agencies had amassed extensive information about Noriega's drug-trafficking for a decade before he was indicted. In 1976, when President Bush was then Director of the CIA, the agency discovered that Noriega had recruited several U.S. Army sergeants as spies. Mr. Bush declined to involve himself with the sergeants, saying that the decision was outside of his jurisdiction, and the sergeants were never prosecuted.

When aiding the Contras was forbidden by Congress, several of the companies used to supply them with arms and weapons were registered in Panama, and, perhaps by coincidence, the legal work was done by General Noriega's lawyer.

In sum, dating back two decades or more Panama had become a focal point for money-laundering, illegal trade in arms and drugs, and espionage (Engelberg & Gerth, 1990).

Writing about what might be termed the widespread, institutionalized corruption and multinational systemic crime in Panama after 1968, when General Omar Torrijos seized power from that country's traditional oligarchy, Frederick Kempe points out:

> From only twelve banks before the 1968 coup, the number expanded to more than 100 by the mid-1970s. Illicit funds flowing to Panama grew commensurately, and dummy corporations multiplied like rabbits. . . . Imediately, Panama became a place where corporations and individuals parked illegal money. Noriega might never have been anymore than a somewhat sadistic and relatively small-time military strongman if it hadn't been for the Panamanian banking system. . . .

> After the Torrijos coup, Panama began replacing pre-Castro Cuba as a magnet for Mafia money laundering, drug racketeering, arms smuggling, and various other contraband operations, ranging from the repacking of embargoed Cuban shrimp under Panamanian coverings for the U.S. market to falsifying end-user certificates in order to pass

American high technology to Castro. . . . the amount of money and
business that would pass through Panama in the 1970s would dwarf that
of pre-Castro Havana. (Kempe, 1990, pp. 74-75) (See also Dinges, 1990)

Clearly, Panama had become an international center for a variety
of state-organized crimes. In fact it seems accurate to state that the
Panamanian government itself had become a major criminal enterprise. During the 20 years following the 1969 coup, the United States
government had repeatedly protected Noriega and his system from
exposure and prosecution, while at the same time using him for its
own clandestine purposes.

This useful "bargain with the devil" might have continued had it
not been for the Iran-Contra scandal of 1986-1987, which exposed so
much that had long been hidden from public view, including Noriega's
relationship with the Contras. This, plus Noriega's two highly publicized indictments on drug charges in a United States that was already
grossly alarmed over its drug problem, appears to have made Noriega's
removal inevitable (Dinges, 1990, pp. 418-423).

In August 1989 the Attorney General of the United States issued
a report (previously discussed in Chapter 3) that identified drug-
trafficking as the number one crime problem facing both the country
and the world. Drawing on reports from the 93 U.S. Attorneys, it
documented the pervasiveness of drug-trafficking throughout the
country. It provided a new portrait of domestic organized crime as it
is being expanded by drug-trafficking conglomerates, including Colombian cartels, Asian Triads, Mexican foreign nationals, and Jamaican posses, operating in various parts of the country, often in close
cooperation with the more established La Cosa Nostra (LCN) and
the Sicilian Mafia crime groups. The Attorney General's report made
very clear that drug-trafficking is not the only systemic criminal activity
of this new and emergent form of transnational crime, operating in
a vast network reaching from this country's inner cities to Latin
America, the Far East, Europe, and other parts of the world. Most visible is the calculated violence of some of these groups, both overseas
and in the United States. Although some groups are also involved in
gun-trafficking, the most marked linkage to other crime patterns is the
relationship of the drug-traffickers to such more traditional organized

crime activities as gambling, extortion, and loan-sharking. Especially significant is the corruption of law enforcement and other officials, the transportation industry, business people and bankers who launder money, and attorneys who aid and abet traffickers.

The following case material describes Asian organized crime groups operating in the United States. Much is known about such groups, but as the Attorney General's report states, much is also not yet known.

Only since the middle 1980s have Asian gangs become a major force in the illicit heroin market in the United States. The gangs, primarily of Chinese origin, are operating on both coasts and are major players in drug-trafficking. Chinese Organized Crime (COC) leaders in this country have used their ties with Far Eastern criminal groups as a source of supply for their illegal markets in video cassettes, prostitutes, drugs, and so forth.

By 1980 Asian-Americans had become the largest immigrant group entering this country. Like other immigrant groups in history, the new Asians tend to be young, know little English, and see organized crime as a quick road to success. There are two main types of Chinese Organized Crime groups in the United States today: American-based COC groups; and Triads, based primarily in Hong Kong, but also in Taiwan. There are perhaps 100,000 Triad members in Hong Kong. The Triads in Taiwan have smaller memberships, with perhaps one gang having 15,000 members worldwide. Only a few Triads are active in North America. There are many similarities between COC groups and La Cosa Nostra (LCN). Both grew out of much older secret or fraternal societies, organized in seventeenth-century China and southern Italy, respectively. Another type of Chinese group, the Tongs, began in the nineteenth century as fraternal organizations for Chinese immigrants brought to the United States. Most American Tongs still serve legitimate business purposes, although several are closely tied to organized crime. Both the COC and the LCN groups place strong emphasis on family ties and on in-group loyalty, with swift retribution against those who inform to outsiders. Both use various subgroups controlled by powerful leaders, and both exercise independence from parent groups overseas. Both COC and LCN groups practice extortion, corruption of public officials, and exploitation of their own innocent, non-English-speaking immigrants. Finally, both engage in a broad range of criminal activities of which drug-trafficking is but one part.

COC groups that have evolved from street gangs among recent Chinese immigrants represent a much greater criminal threat than the Triads. Although not operating on the same large scale as the Colombian cartels, Chinese Organized Crime groups in America are the largest importers of heroin from Southeast Asia. COC groups operate mainly as shippers and wholesalers of heroin, apparently working through other groups, especially the LCN in this country, to distribute the drug to users. Although Hong Kong-based Triads are also involved in drug-trafficking, their exact roles are not clear.

There is a huge, growing inflow of money from Hong Kong, Taipei, and Singapore banks, primarily to banks in San Francisco, Los Angeles, and New York. Some of these funds flow to large American commercial banks, with the rest going into some 100 Chinese-owned-and-operated American banks. Much of this money is legitimate, but inconspicuously mixed into this wide stream of funds are the profits from drug-trafficking. These profits are frequently invested in such U.S. real estate holdings as shopping centers, apartment complexes, office buildings, nightclubs, restaurants, travel agencies, and so on. Many of these serve to launder additional legal and illegal cash.[1]

A careful reading of the Attorney General's report strongly suggests that what happened during Prohibition in the United States is happening again, this time with illegal drugs. Back then, Irish, Jewish, Italian, and other immigrant groups had become involved in Prohibition, and this had contributed in a major way to the rapid expansion of organized crime. As a consequence of the profits made during Prohibition, and the growth of large ethnic organized crime families who became increasingly sophisticated in methods of corruption, organized crime in the United States became extremely powerful, diversified, and institutionalized. What appears to be occurring now, as suggested by an interpretation of the Attorney General's report, is that new immigrant groups from Asia, Latin America, the Caribbean, and to a lesser degree Africa, as well as indigenous American gangs, may be following the same historical route with the large amounts of money earned from drug-trafficking. Organized crime among these groups is following the traditional pattern: Diversification of criminal and non-criminal economic activities appears to be happening; widespread experience with corruption of public officials essential for the prosperity of organized crime is becoming common; and the quick use of violence for business purposes has become the norm. If heroin, cocaine, and other illegal drugs should some day be decriminalized, or if the market demand for such drugs in the United States should sharply decline, as it did between 1920 and 1960 (Musto, 1987, pp. 251-253), there is the very real possibility that the multinational drug-trafficking organizations may not disappear or suddenly turn to entirely legitimate economic activities. Instead, it is very possible that such organizations may expand farther into other organized criminal enterprises, both domestic and multinational. In sum, the phenomenal growth in the demand for illegal drugs in the United States since the 1960s may have provided a window of economic opportunity for new immigrant groups to enter the organized crime marketplace and become established.

IDEOLOGY, THEORY, AND RESTRAINTS
ON CRIME CONTROL POLICY

It is sharply evident from the history of the study of domestic crime that such efforts have consistently raised problems of definition, have developed many issues about the acceptability of theories of causation, and have produced a wide variety of recurring policy debates about prevention and control. Typically, such problems, issues, and debates have not been settled by simply "weighing the scientific evidence" or "by letting the data speak for themselves." At bottom, the dominant values and interests of a society set what its political system will outlaw as crime; different theories of crime causation will come and go, depending on the temper and style of the times; and different policies of crime prevention and control will rise or fall as a society's value orientation and priority of interests shift and change over time. To illustrate briefly: Nontherapeutic abortion will be a crime at one time, but not at another; "opportunity theory" will be the rage in a liberal decade, but will be replaced by conservative "deterrence theory" in another; and rehabilitation and job training will be in style as public policy in one generation, but rigorous punishment and imprisonment will be back in fashion again in another. Such changes do not appear to occur simply because of scientific advancements in society's knowledge base about crime, criminals, and prevention and control. They apparently occur because of shifts in society's values and political priorities (Barlow, 1990, pp. 28-29; Radzinowicz, 1966; Williams & McShane, 1988, p. 7).

Based on this principle, it would appear important for criminology and criminal justice to recognize at once that any study of the four multinational crime systems examined in this book is especially prone to being tilted by the particular relationship, identification, or empathy the examiner has with various world views, especially with the nation-states or other groups involved in such crimes as victims, collaborators, or perpetrators. Values and political interests impact on much of what is written regarding domestic crime; they may impact even more vigorously on much of what is written about the types of multinational crime under discussion, when the stakes are often geopolitical and subject to the strongest possible conflicts arising out of fundamental differences in the history, ideology, and resources of the nation-states or other groups involved.

One simple illustration should be helpful in making this principle more clearly understood. In reviewing the literature on modern terrorism, it will be easy to recognize various statements which maintain, for example, that the political violence against established governments perpetrated by the Irish Republican Army, the Palestine Liberation Organization, the African National Congress, or Afghan rebels is justified, while other statements condemn as terrorism the same political violence by the same groups against exactly the same established governments. Same groups, same political violence, same established governments, but sharply conflicting judgments arising from the sharply conflicting values and interests of different observers. Thus, as was discussed in the Introduction, what a nation defines as "terrorism" may depend much more on that nation's political interests than on some intrinsic quality of the violence being judged.[2]

It should be clear from the above that criminological theory does not develop in a social vacuum. Instead, it reflects the beliefs and values of not only the cultural context within which the theory is articulated but also the cultural context within which the criminologist presenting the theory has been socialized. In brief, the cultural context provides the ideological frame of reference that influences the criminologist's theoretical formulations.

Three competing ideological perspectives may be said to characterize criminology (Barlow, 1990, pp. 29-31):

Conservative Criminology. The causes of crime are located in the characteristics of the individuals who commit them. The "right" questions to ask are: How are such morally defective individuals produced? and How can society protect itself against them? The solution to the crime problem is seen in terms of a return to basic values wherein good wins over evil. Until early in the twentieth century, most criminological theory was conservative.

Liberal Criminology. This perspective began to emerge in criminology during the later 1930s and early 1940s, and it soon became dominant. The most influential versions of liberal criminology explain criminal behavior either in terms of the way society is organized (social structure), or in terms of the way people acquire social attributes (social process). Conflict theory illustrates a structural perspective, and social learning theory is an example of social process.

Radical Criminology. Whereas liberal criminologists do not call for basic changes in the economic institutions of society, radical criminologists view such changes as mandatory. In rejecting the liberal tradition, radicals believe that crime and criminality are manifestations of the exploitative character of monopoly capitalism. Radical criminology became an influence in the 1970s.

The impact of these three ideological positions on American crime policy has been very mixed. Radical criminology has had little or no impact. Liberal criminology has had a moderate impact in its efforts to establish practices of fair and just treatment by police, the courts, and prisons. But the dominant influence on public policy for several recent decades has been that of conservative criminology.

This policy has given rise to what has been called the "crime control model" of criminal justice (Siegel, 1986, pp. 461-464). This pays the most attention to the capacity of the criminal justice system to apprehend, prosecute, convict, and dispose of a high proportion of criminal offenders. A premium is placed on speed and finality and a presumption that those apprehended by the police are in fact guilty. The extensive use of plea bargaining rather than trials is encouraged. Efficiency, productivity, and professionalism are emphasized. The focus is on establishing order through efficient legal repression. Serious offenders, especially street criminals, should receive swift and certain punishment. Even government-funded criminal justice research in the 1970s was reflective of the conservative bent of national crime policy, with its emphasis on deterrence, career criminals, prosecution, and sentencing. This conservative perspective in government-funded criminal justice research has continued through the 1980s. The National Institute of Justice Research Program Plan for 1989, for example, announced grant money available for such topics as: the apprehension, prosecution, and adjudication of criminal offenders; public safety and security; punishment and control of offenders; criminal careers and the control of crime; and violent criminal behavior (U.S. Department of Justice, 1988).

This very brief review of the dominant position of the crime control model in national criminal justice policy suggests that a very serious dislocation exists between contemporary theory in academic criminology and present criminal justice policy and practice. Liberal criminology, influenced by a liberal ideology, was dominant in academic criminology by the end of World War II, perhaps somewhat earlier. It apparently remains so today. It may be inferred that the current crime control model of criminal justice has its intellectual roots in the conservative "criminological theory" of the eighteenth century. This was influenced by a conservative ideology and a growing scientific positivism, which, increasingly through the nineteenth and twentieth centuries, focused the theory's attention not on social structure or on social process, but on the moral and other "defects" of individual criminals, and on legal repression. Without digressing to go into detail about the many possible consequences of this dislocation, it is perhaps sufficient to state the following. There is, of course, no way of currently knowing if a different criminal justice policy, based perhaps on liberal criminological theory, would be more efficient in controlling the domestic crime problem in the United States than is the present policy, based on conservative ideology and theory. Such a policy might be more efficient, or it might not. We simply do not have at hand the scientific tools to settle the question. In point of fact, perhaps we are never likely to really know. The matter will probably continue to be settled not on the basis of firm empirical evidence—as is also the case with so many other pressing social issues—but on the basis of values, interests, and political influence. And it seems clear that liberal academic criminologists simply do not now have a strong enough political constituency to displace those who support current conservative criminal justice arrangements.

Vold and Bernard (1986, p. 355) put the matter in the following terms:

> Here, then, is the heart of the problem between criminology theory and crime policy. Criminology theory attempts to explain the basic problem of crime. In so doing it looks at any number of different variables, from those associated with the individual offender to those associated with the political and economic systems of the society itself. Crime policies can be derived from all aspects of criminology theory, but only policies that do not disturb the larger group interests can be implemented. Thus only those policies derived from criminology theories that focus on offenders and their immediate environments can be implemented, and only to the extent that the larger social arrangements are not disturbed. . . . Criminological theory has no such limitation. . . . The end result is an impasse in which the policy implications of most criminology theories are never implemented and criminology itself is viewed as having little or nothing practical to say about crime policy.

There is perhaps at least one major geopolitical difficulty in applying to the problem of multinational systemic crime a conservative criminal justice policy—a policy that was developed to deal with domestic individual criminals largely of a conventional type. To apprehend, prosecute, convict, and imprison individual street criminals from America's inner cities is one sort of task, difficult and expensive as it may be. It would appear to be a much more difficult assignment to identify, locate, and successfully engage the various multinational private and government organizations, groups, and aligned individuals related to espionage, terrorism, arms-trafficking, and drug-trafficking as each system impacts on the United States. That such social collectivities may be powerful, clandestine, and operating out of distant and diverse foreign regions of the world would seem to complicate the task even further. Moreover, representatives of the United States government may not be entirely welcome in some of the nations found in these various regions. This would seem to be especially true for U.S. law enforcement agents assigned to investigate foreign indigenous organizations, groups, and perhaps government officials involved in significant multinational crime systems that the U. S. government has decided are a threat to its security.

Perhaps the following example will make this point clearer. Southwest Asia is home to much opium production, where Afghanistan, Iran, and Pakistan are heavily involved in the growing of opium poppies. In the mid-1980s, Pakistan was reported to have a large number of heroin-trafficking organizations with a well-entrenched distribution infrastructure in the Arabian Gulf, Europe, and North America. In Afghanistan the Mujahadeen freedom fighters were reported to control 80% of the rural areas, and it was within these areas that the majority of poppy crops and heroin laboratories were located (Royal Canadian Mounted Police, 1988). Obviously, perhaps, it would be difficult for United States authorities to implement the indictment, apprehension, extradition, and trial in the United States of drug-lords from Southwest Asia. Afghanistan, Iran, and, to a degree, Pakistan are clearly not within this nation's sphere of geopolitical influence in either the same sense or to the same degree as are some Central American and South American cocaine transit and source countries. There have been indictments of a few cocaine drug-lords and they have been removed to the United States for trial, but at the cost of great violence in the two countries most involved, Colombia and Panama. Whether the political gains from such a policy will offset the political costs of the death and destruction wrought in Panama and Colombia remains an open question. It may take years or decades to make a proper assessment.

What seems more certain at the moment is this: The same foreign policy perhaps could not at present be applied by the United States to Afghanistan, Iran, and Pakistan, for example, without risking major international discord and possibly even a protracted war on the Asian mainland. Central America and South America, particularly those parts bordering the Caribbean Basin, are one geopolitical arena; Southwest Asia appears to be quite another. Moreover, it may even be very difficult for U.S. authorities to effect extradition of defendants from neighboring Mexico, a major source of illegal drugs for northern markets. Mexico is reported to have an almost universal policy of refusing to extradite its own citizens to the United States, and on at least one occasion refused to extradite across the border a U.S. citizen wanted on terrorism charges (Rohter, 1990). This suggests that even with a high level of concern in the United States about imported illegal drugs, the present conservative crime control model, especially if it involves extradition, has only limited overseas applicability for dealing with the problem of drug-trafficking.

For much the same reasons, the model may also have only limited applicability as a policy for controlling other types of multinational systemic crime. Yet as late as 1988, a ranking spokesman for the U.S. Department of State maintained that the stated policy of the United States for preventing terrorism where American interests are at stake involved efforts to identify, track, apprehend, prosecute, and punish terrorists; prosecution and punishment not only get individual terrorists off the streets, but such a program also deters others.[3] As with the punishment of foreign drug-lords, this also requires a good deal of cooperation from foreign nation-states where terrorists may either reside or be citizens. In the Middle East, Iran and Syria have been most successful at using terrorism as an instrument of their foreign policy. With the threat of terrorism, Iran has successfully established a wide sphere of influence in its part of the world. Many nations there, including Pakistan and Turkey, accommodate to Iran's wishes, and Western influence has been substantially reduced. Syria, too, has used terrorism successfully as part of its foreign policy. Through the threat of its use, Arab states have been persuaded to be less accommodating toward Israel. Terrorism helps Damascus control most of Lebanon. It boosts an otherwise frail alliance with Libya and Iran. It helps destabilize Turkey, a key member of the North Atlantic Treaty Alliance. And state-supported terrorism from Syria dominates the Jordanian government (Pipes, 1988).

Against this sustained and successful use of terrorism, the United States maintains its efforts to punish the agents of state-organized Iranian and Syrian terrorism, as well as other terrorists who act against its interests. But certainly it seems fair to conclude that the United States should not expect to identify, track, apprehend, prosecute, and punish many terrorists residing within Iran and Syria, or within the effective sphere of influence of these two nation-states, as long as hostility and conflict mark the relations between the United States and these two countries.

This suggests a more general test that might be applied when evaluating any policy developed by the United States that requires the cooperation of foreign states to control multinational crime impacting on this country from overseas. Specifically, does a policy requiring substantial cooperation make sense in the full cultural, economic, and political context of the international "setting" (Louis Kriesberg's concept described in the Introduction) in which it is to be tried? Are the relationships with the United States, as well as the political, economic, and other national interests of the foreign countries involved, such that commitment to and participation in the American policy seem likely? Or, to put the matter another way, if vital aspects of multinational crime violating American interests arise out of the national political and/or economic interests of a foreign power or its close allies, how much cooperation with American control policies is likely to be forthcoming? Needless to say, before this tack on evaluation of policy can be undertaken successfully, considerable knowledge has to be acquired regarding the particulars of the foreign nations involved, their relationships with one another, and their relationships with the United States. Given the requirements of the interactionist perspective (also described in the Introduction), definitions of the prevailing situations, as perceived by significant actors in the foreign countries involved, form a crucial dimension in any effort at understanding how such countries are likely to react to American policy initiatives. Definitions by outsiders, including Americans, may be far less related to actual outcomes. Yet outside definitions are almost certain to prevail in setting policy if they not only are derived from but also reinforce vital outside national values and political interests. In a worst-case scenario, when outside definitions either dominate or ignore definitions held by significant actors in the nations whose cooperation is required, the possibility for a failed policy becomes likely. Perhaps it is through the actual empirical study of circumstances such as these that the impact of values and interests on international crime control policies, and their success or failure, might become more evident.

NATIONAL SECURITY RESTRAINTS ON RESEARCH

The relationship of national security to the problems of doing research about multinational systemic crime is illustrated by the evasion, the secrecy, and the lack of interest George Thayer encountered in writing his book, *The War Business: The International Trade in Armaments* (1969). Thayer describes the massive proliferation of conventional weapons of war following World War II and the vast legal and illegal trade in these weapons from both democratic and Communist countries to various client states throughout the Third World. Despite the outbreaks of war, revolution, and other hostilities encouraged by this arms trade, Thayer found little literature on the subject, no interest at the United Nations, and few academics giving attention to the topic. In addition, few government officials would talk about the subject and most claimed that materials about the arms trade were "classified." The Soviets and the Czechs were stunned by having questions asked about the subject. U. S. military and civilian intelligence officers evaded Thayer's questions, and most were unwilling to discuss even unclassified aspects of the trade.

Thayer concluded that no one wanted to control the trade in conventional arms. The United States, the Soviet Union, China, and other producing nations had more than their national security at stake; selling arms helped to balance national budgets, reduced trade deficits, created friends, strengthened alliances, and so on.

Thayer's conclusion suggests the possibility, tentative as it may be, that when government agencies evade or reject requests to cooperate with research about multinational crime, such agencies may be doing far more than protecting ongoing criminal investigations, legitimate sources, and intelligence methods. They may also be protecting their own wrongdoing or that of others. The Iran-Contra Affair (Inouye & Hamilton, 1988) and the case of General Manuel Antonio Noriega, the former leader of Panama (Kempe, 1990), illustrate how secrecy may be used by agencies of government to conceal behavior that is contrary to law, or unambiguously criminal. In Iran-Contra the Contra rebels were resupplied by President Ronald Reagan's National Security Council staff when such resupply was forbidden by law, and the alleged drug-trafficking of General Noriega was reportedly obscured by various U.S. intelligence agencies over the years because he was then considered to be a valuable intelligence asset. In the first instance, secrecy enabled the Office of the President to evade the Boland Amendment imposed by Congress; in the second, the protection afforded by intelligence agencies may well have delayed both indictments of Noriega and others by U.S. Attorneys and the investigations of the Drug Enforcement Administration into drug-trafficking in Central America.

The protection apparently afforded Noriega was not unique. In foreign affairs the domestic drug problem often takes second place to other major American foreign policy goals. Thus, as David Musto (1987, p. 256) puts it:

> As bad as drug-trafficking might appear to Americans, when a decision involves dealing effectively with a drug-producing or exporting nation while maintaining national security interests through friendly relations with that country, national security and good relations nearly always win out over the important but less crucial issue of drugs.

The situation in Afghanistan in 1990 provides a vivid illustration of how the foreign policy interests of the United States can override the country's concern about reducing the influx of illegal drugs from overseas. Although both the U. S. government and American reporters covering the Afghan war knew for years about the involvement of Afghan rebels in opium-trafficking, both were often silent about the subject, even though the United States was the principal supplier of arms to the rebels. Thus:

> [W]hile they continued to receive American arms, (some rebels) turned their energies toward a burgeoning trade in opium, a traditional Afghan enterprise that grew so rapidly in rebel-held areas that the country now exports at least 800 tons, perhaps as many as 2,000, of opium gum a year—figures which, according to American drug enforcement officials, place Afghanistan second only to the "golden triangle" of Burma,

Thailand and Laos as the world's largest source of the raw material for heroin. . . .

Most of the opium is processed in laboratories in rebel areas, or shipped—generally aboard donkeys, but sometimes aboard jeeps bought with United States funds—to processing plants in Pakistan.

According to official American estimates, perhaps proportions of the heroin—tons every year, worth billions of dollars on the street—is eventually sold in the United States, accounting for perhaps one in three heroin deals in the country. . . .

For Americans, the enormous growth in the heroin trade may be the most lasting consequence of the war. Yet American officials made little of it in public until recent months. (Burns, 1990)

Further illustration may be helpful: Thayer points out the extensive role bribery plays in doing business in the "Bribery Belt" for arms dealers, bankers, salespeople, even tourists (Thayer, 1969, pp. 126-130). In this part of the world, "from Manila to Bangkok, from Rangoon to Cairo, from Casablanca to Sao Paulo, bribery is a way of life; it is habitual, ubiquitous and, in places, traditional" (Thayer, 1969, p. 127). It seems fair to presume that no government agency is likely to admit easily to such facts when it has knowledge of bribery being used, for example, in selling its country's arms through private dealers to client states in the Third World. Many tactics might be employed by an agency to avoid revealing such bribery, including closing out inquiry by citing the need to protect national security.

These illustrations seem to make clear that, in the area of international affairs, the various agencies of a government simply may not share the same policy priorities. In terms of the present discussion, some may not place their highest priority on obeying the law, or on providing to their counterparts in law enforcement information they have regarding crimes or other wrongdoing. The illustrations further suggest that "national security" may be used both as a legitimate policy goal and as a defense against revealing compromising information to outsiders.

At this point it needs to be made clear that the denial of cooperation in the investigation of multinational crime may go far beyond a government's refusal to provide information for the purposes of academic research. Such refusal may also involve the refusal of one government to cooperate with another in a major criminal investigation, not for reasons of national security but for the far more limited and self-serving reason of protecting particular officials, industrial leaders, and others from embarrassment, scandal, and possible charges of criminal behavior.

The following case is illustrative:

> In early 1990 the government of India opened a criminal investigation into allegations of official corruption in a 1986 weapons purchase by the Indian Army. The Indian government purchased 410 field howitzers from Bofors, the Swedish arms manufacturer.
>
> The Indian and Swedish press reported that Indian government officials at the time appeared to have taken part in a cover-up of multimillion-dollar commissions paid to middle men on the $1.4-billion arms sale. It was alleged that some of the commission money was used to bribe Indian officials to award the contract to Bofors. The press also said Indian politicians and Swedish officials were party to discussions trying to conceal the illegal payments. The investigation sought to have Bofors name the recipients of the illegal payments.
>
> Indian officials said Sweden had not been cooperative in pursuing the investigation, possibly because high Swedish officials as well as industrial leaders could have been exposed and embarrassed, if not charged with criminal behavior.[4]

When government officials cite national security as a reason for not providing information for academic or other investigative purposes, the question of motive remains unresolved. This would seem to be the case particularly when the information requested bears on the possible embarrassing or criminal behavior of public officials, business executives, and others close to the centers of power in the government denying the request. It may also reflect not simply individual deviancy but also the policy position that one or more agencies in the government may wish to keep secret.

In the study of multinational systemic crime, the denial of information by government raises the possibility of a cover-up by special interests and is suggestive of a possible relationship that either government itself or individual officials may have to the criminal system being investigated. If such a relationship does exist, then a crucial further question arises: Is the relationship an instrument of agency policy or is it the isolated behavior of a few "bad apples" in the system? Obviously, a defense strategy for an agency publicly caught in a relationship with a multinational crime system is to maximize the ambiguity about the exact degree and depth of its involvement. According to this defense strategy, if organizational damage is to be minimized, "corporate" responsibility must to be denied at all costs.

However, to turn over deviant members to external authorities, instead of shielding them in some way and then subjecting them to discrete internal sanctions, does little to promote the collective integrity of the parent group (Katz, 1977). Thus, for sensitive government agencies it would appear much more productive in the organizational sense to "stretch" if need be the legitimate use and application of the term *national security* to protect both itself and its deviant members from outside review and then apply to such members discreet internal sanctions.

NOTES

1   Adapted from the U.S. Attorney General's Report (August 1989).

2. For a discussion of the complicated nature of terrorism from the point of view of value judgments, see Long (1990).

3. This policy was stated by Bremer (1988), Ambassador at Large for Counter-Terrorism, U.S. Department of State, addressing the Conference of Middle East Fundamentalism and Terrorism, The Carnegie Endowment for International Peace, April 21, 1988.

4. Adapted from Crossette, (1990).

5

Approaching the Study of Multinational Systemic Crime

At best we are in the earliest stages of the scientific study of multinational systemic crime. Even descriptive facts about such crime are in short supply, especially data drawn from field studies in the natural settings in which such crime occurs (on this point more generally, see Polsky, 1967). The development of more facts awaits the results of future research. This chapter will not attempt to apply the scientific method to the study of multinational systemic crime, nor will it present a theory to explain such crime or offer recommendations about its control. There appears to be too little known, both empirically and theoretically, about such behavior to attempt these tasks here. Before serious theory construction can fruitfully begin, and policy recommendations based on such theory follow, many more descriptive facts about multinational systemic crime will have to be developed by additional research.

At this point some effort has been made to identify the concept of multinational systemic crime and describe several types of such behavior. Observations have also been made regarding understanding and coping with such behavior systems. Basic data necessary for the valid and reliable descriptions of such systems—including their organizations, behavior, participants, and the contexts in which they rise and decline—are not yet at hand. In sum, we are still far from that stage of scientific investigation where we can begin to assemble valid and reliable descriptive facts and establish and explain relationships in order to construct theories regarding multinational systemic crime and its subtypes. And without empirically grounded theory, policies for the control of such crime become matters of belief and pragmatic commitment, not science.

PROBLEMS IN THEORY CONSTRUCTION
AND POLICY DEVELOPMENT

Threatened by multinational crime, national leaders appear to develop and implement policies of control, not on the basis of scientifically derived theory, but on the basis of their ideologies, political interests, or pure pragmatism. The policies and programs often occur first, perhaps followed by some unverifiable theoretical rationale.

Perhaps the less said here about such public policies, the better, since no nation-state has as yet been able to rid itself of such problems or to even demonstrate that it has matters under a reasonable degree of control. However, it is important to note that national leaders faced with such pressing problems cannot postpone taking action until some theory of causation is developed through the application of the scientific method. The wait may be far too long. Besides, there are so many different theories of crime causation presently being debated by criminologists and others, that the development of a widely accepted one about the causes of multinational systemic crime is not likely to soon occur. Even if a theory should eventually become available and win widespread support, control policies based on it might be judged too complex or risky or expensive to implement; they might require action that runs counter to other more important foreign policy priorities of a nation; or such policies might simply be found unacceptable because of strong ideological reasons.

Of all the reasons why a theory and control policies derived from it might be rejected, none appears to be more powerful than those arising out of ideology. The ideological climate of a society can make or break the public's acceptance of both a crime causation theory and a control policy. For this reason, and for the reason of sound science, any theory advanced about multinational systemic crime should be based on a substantial data base. Yet the weight of the scientific evidence supporting crime causation theories is not likely to be so compelling that there is no room for considerable doubt. Moreover, the type of evidence selected and the type ignored are themselves influenced by the investigator's orientation, both theoretical and ideological. The relationship of ideology to criminological theory and crime control policy has been discussed more extensively in Chapter 4. It is sufficient here to reaffirm the power of the ideological climate of a society to influence the acceptance or rejection of causal theory and control policy in the area of criminological thought. Nonetheless, it is perhaps useful to suggest that efforts at "marketing" a theory about multinational systemic crime await the availability of an ample empirically derived data base to support an argument for its acceptance. What should be avoided is the presentation of an explanation and a solution that are based on anger and scant data or no data at all. In another context, writing about the complex relationship between the military and the state in Latin America, Alain Rouquié (1987, p. 2) has put the issue in these terms:

> With the help of angry participant-observers, ingenious and unverifiable theories (appear). These universally applicable explanations or keys to the universe are merely more or less coherent extrapolations based on fragile or spectacular evidence. They serve to set out some guidelines in an area in which great confusion reigns, precisely because of the lack of serious empirical study; however, they also reassure those who accept them. Successive interpretations emerge at each stage, adjusting themselves to the contemporary situation. Models bloom and fade. A new orthodoxy eliminates an earlier one, which in turn re-emerges a little later in a more sophisticated and equally convincing form that is both coherent and applicable, but often neither true nor false.

The task of developing a theory and a control policy relative to such behavior is complicated even more by the fact that various subtypes of multinational systemic crime are also often interrelated in various ways, as was also discussed in Chapter 4. Terrorism, drug-trafficking, and arms-trafficking, sometimes also espionage, all occurring at the same time in the same geographical arena and involving the same or sometimes different groups, is a most complex dependent variable to explain. Where and under what circumstances and environmental conditions do such configurations occur? What is the nature of the interaction between different groups engaged in such behaviors? In a world of booming multinational crime, are there emerging ecological patterns to such interrelated criminal systems? These and many other relevant questions require difficult empirical answers if factually based theories are to be constructed. And the problem of developing, applying, and evaluating a control policy presents its own dilemmas and dangers. To reduce successfully the danger from one form of multi-national crime may sometimes serve to increase the threat of another. For example, to destroy the drug crops in a Third World area without adequate compensation to the peasant growers is likely to increase their discontent and possibly drive them closer to the ranks of local insurgent or terrorist factions. This might serve to increase the level of violence and the need for an increase in the flow of illegal weapons to sustain it. On the other hand, to provide the peasant growers with large cash subsidies not to grow drugs may give them more cash on hand than formerly, especially if they continue to grow drugs anyway. Such an increased cash flow might easily lead to an increase in the "taxes" for protection levied on the growers by local insurgent or terrorist groups. Such groups could then use the increased revenue to expand their ranks, increase their need for illegal weapons, and escalate their violence against the government. The point is that insurgency or ter-rorism costs money. Any large increase in narco-related cash to a poli-tically unstable drug-producing area is likely to be appropriated by those who have the guns. With it they are likely to buy more guns.

The case of Peru in early 1990 illustrates such a possibility. Peru was described as the Latin America country that had become impov-erished the fastest during the previous 30 years. During 1988 and 1989, Peru's official economy shrank by 20%. Guerrilla groups were very active. During 1989 political killings jumped 60%, to 3,198, about half of which were attributed to the Shining Path, a Maoist-inspired guerrilla group that had a profitable alliance with traffick-ers of Peru's largest export—cocaine. The coca-leaf harvest, which was the world's largest, was believed to inject as much as $1 billion into Peru's economy each year (Brooke, 1990a). Coca clearly was that country's cash crop. The U.S. State Department reported that in 1989 Peru produced 124,208 metric tons of coca leaf, more than Bolivia, Colombia, and Ecuador combined (Sciolino, 1990).

A Peruvian regular army general responsible for the security of one large up-country coca-producing valley reported that coca was the guerrilla's lifeblood. He went on to state:

> The guerrillas have protected the growers and make sure they receive a good price for their crop; in return the guerrillas have levied a 5 to 15 percent "tax" on the earnings. They also charge the traffickers up to $15,000 for each flight into the region. All told, the insurgents have been earning perhaps $30 million a year from coca, enabling them to spread their operations throughout Peru (Massing, 1990).

This same general estimated that to really develop his valley and solve its coca problem would cost about $3 billion. It is interesting to compare this amount with the $3.1 million the United States allotted in 1990 for economic assistance to all of Peru (Massing, 1990).

The matter of economic assistance as a method of reducing coca production can be debated endlessly. The basic point is that cash assistance to coca farmers may also be indirect cash assistance to local guerrilla forces when the two coexist in the same geographic area.

Mark S. Steinitz (1985) presents an informative description of the interrelationships between terrorists, drug-traffickers, and illegal arms in various drug source areas of the world. He notes that the drug trade, insurgency, terrorism, and the need for illegal small arms tend to be located in roughly the same areas of the world. Such areas include Latin America, Southeast Asia, South Asia, and the Middle East among others. The worldwide expansion in the use of drugs has brought a flood of hard currency to these areas that helps support not only the drug-traffickers but also those engaged in insurgency and terrorism. Thus, in various areas of the world, drugs, terrorism, and arms appear to have a kind of symbiotic relationship, which has been described in these terms:

> For insurgents and terrorists, the drug trade offers sums of money that would tempt the most ardent Marxist-Leninist. For traffickers, who live in a world where the threat of violence is constant, insurgents and terrorists offer much needed sources of protection and an enforcement capability. Aside from this there are several other items that insurgents, terrorists, and traffickers are constantly searching for: arms, clandestine transportation and methods of communication, corrupt officials,

false documentation, and information on the activities of police and security forces. (Steinitz, 1985)

Peter Lupsha (1988) suggests drug-trafficking may play a central role in financing both rebels and loyalists in some of the "invisible wars" of liberation and repression now characteristic of the Third World. Arms-trafficking, terrorism, guerrilla warfare, as well as the violence and other illegal activities of governments may all be paid for and enhanced by the wealth and resources of drug-traffickers. Seen in this way, readily available narco-dollars may finance all kinds of political groups in their struggles for power in underdeveloped regions (Long, 1990, pp. 115-118). Backed by their wealth, organizational resources, and capacity for violence, drug-traffickers may possibly be forming alliances, consolidating power, and gradually emerging as a new entrepreneurial elite in the drug source regions of the Third World.[1] If, in fact, this is occurring (and much research is needed to test this proposition), what obstacles would such developments raise for effective drug-control policy? What policy can control drug-trafficking in parts of the world where organized traffickers exercise significant political power?[2]

Moreover, although it is commonly assumed to be true, there appears to be no valid reason for concluding that drug wealth only corrupts and destabilizes a nation's social institutions. As with other kinds of wealth, narco-dollars, particularly after they have been successfully laundered, may in fact be used for a variety of legitimate purposes, including capital investments, relief for the poor, and the financing of political parties. One contemporary illustration of how drug money can contribute to a nation's economic and political stability is found in an economic analysis of Bolivia published in 1991. Bolivia is described as a country with a sad and turbulent history that continues to repeat itself: It is now in the midst of a cocaine boom, which has replaced the tin boom of the previous century, which in turn replaced the exploitation of silver and other precious metals of the colonial period. Today in Bolivia, "while the coca farmer makes a living, the cocaine trafficker makes a killing." Coca production and trade dominate the Bolivian economy, accounting for 66% of its export earnings. The huge profits made from cocaine have led to widespread corruption in Bolivian politics, and the battle against the peasant coca-producers and the cocaine-traffickers is making little progress. But in the center of all of this, drug money is laundered and deposited in Bolivian banks in such large amounts that Bolivia's currency and price levels have stabilized, measured against earlier periods of wild inflation and political turmoil. A kind of "cocaine stabilization" has occurred. New drug entrepreneurs are becoming respectable business people. While the drug-traffickers move toward respectability and legitimacy, the poor Bolivian peasant coca-growers struggle to survive against the armed might of the United States and Bolivian militaries. In 1990 and 1991 U.S. financial aid was designed to finance armed conflict against peasant coca-producers (drug-eradication) and to encourage coca-crop substitution programs. Bolivian drug-money launderers and their bankers were not targets of this United States-supported drug war. In fact, the United States was reported to have encouraged international money-laundering out of Bolivia through foreign banks, including those in the United States and Panama (Burke, 1991).

In the absence of sufficient facts, to assume that narco-dollars cannot serve legitimate purposes is just possibly a good illustration of the problem created when strong negative stereotypes about crime and criminals distort reality.

*   *   *

Many problems beset understanding and coping with multinational systemic crime. Some of these have already been discussed. These include a lack of valid and reliable facts upon which to construct theoretical interpretations (see Becker, 1963), and the impact of ideology on both theory and policy. Another common problem is that the frequent and complex interrelationships between various types of crime complicate specification of the dependent variable in research and present difficult policy dilemmas. Some of these problems seem to be shared with efforts to deal with the crime problem generally. Other problems seem to be unique to the study of multinational crime. The role of "national security" interests in prohibiting the collection of data, as discussed in Chapter 4, appears to be one example of such uniqueness. Another, also discussed in Chapter 4, is the array of different nation-states, each representing a different legal jurisdiction, which are involved in multinational crime, and the problems this presents to the United States for both the evaluation of overseas crime control policies and the practicalities of international law enforcement. Clearly, many other problems exist in the study of multinational crime, but these will not be discussed here.

THREE CONCEPTUAL AND METHODOLOGICAL ORIENTATIONS FOR GUIDING RESEARCH

The remaining sections of this chapter present the outlines of three orientations believed to offer good prospects for the scientific study of multinational crime and eventually for the development of policies to control it. The *first* presents a perspective for the study of the systems or criminal organizations involved in such crime. The *second* sets forth a methodological orientation for applying what has been called the interactionist approach to the study of social life. In this case the objective is to study criminal organizations from the inside, in terms of the meaning behavior has for participants as a product of the social interactions they have with others, both inside and outside their groups. The core of the method requires the direct examination of the actual ongoing social world of subjects in the field as it is lived. The *third* orientation sets forth a model useful for describing actual multinational criminal organizations, in terms of the various stages and other aspects of the conflict relationship in which each is involved; the focus is on describing the struggles between such organizations and those parties outside of and sometimes in violent and sustained conflict with such organizations.

The Study of Criminal Organizations

In their study, titled *Corporate Crime* (1980), Marshall B. Clinard and Peter C. Yeager point out that:

> Even though the law treats corporations as intangible persons, illegal corporate behavior cannot be fully explored within the framework of theories of deviance and crime that are applicable to individuals. Instead, the first step in understanding corporate illegality is to drop the

analogy of the corporation as a person and analyze the behavior of the corporation in terms of what it really is: a complex organization. Within this framework corporate crime is viewed as organization crime.

This organizational perspective is the one that appears best suited to the study of different types of multinational systemic crime, even though such systems are quite different in essential ways from the business corporations studied by Clinard and Yeager. The point is that, for purposes of scientific investigation, the criminal behavior of multinational crime systems is best approached as the behavior of actors meeting one of the goals of complex organizations, not as the behavior of individual criminals. Unfortunately, as Donald R. Cressey points out in his study, *Criminal Organization: Its Elementary Forms* (1972), both the popular and the scientific tendency is to view criminal behavior as a problem rooted in the personalities of individual criminals and not in terms of the organizational arrangements among criminals who act in concert. As a consequence, there are very few descriptions of what the participants in criminal organizations actually do.

Of course, crimes are not typically committed by individuals acting alone. Most crimes are committed by two or more persons behaving within some matrix of social relationships. The study of social relationships and the interactions of actors involved in them who commit crimes may be called the study of criminal organization; the study of the noncriminal behavior of actors involved in another matrix of social relationships, such as a university or a school yard play group, may be called the study of social organization. The difference between the concept of criminal organization and that of social organization is not found in the quality or the degree of organization per se, but in the judgment of competent legal authority as to whether the behavior involved is criminal (see Cohen, 1977).

In the sense that it is used here, most crime is organized to one degree or another, ranging from such informal and transitory relationships as those of the prostitute-client to the large-scale syndicate type of organizations. As is generally true with social organizations, criminal organizations vary widely in size or number of participants, purposes or goals, duration of organizational history, degree of formal organization, and other ways.

The concept of social organization is commonly understood and widely used by both laypeople and social scientists in their descriptions of the social relationships and interactions characteristic of social life. Illustrations abound as, for example, in our references to the social life of family, church, workplace, social club, political party, friendship clique, neighborhood, and so on. Despite this commonplace application of the idea of social organization to everyday life, the companion concept of criminal organization has not commonly been used by the public or by criminologists to describe the social relationships and social interaction among people who commit crime together. In brief, the relationships and interaction among the participants in criminal organizations is seldom discussed. Indeed, the great scarcity of detailed, valid, and reliable descriptive data about how various kinds of criminal organizations actually function—in Cressey's words cited earlier: "what the participants in criminal organizations actually do"—presents a serious obstacle to their scientific study by outside investigaors. Names are often given to criminal organizations, such as the Colombian cartels or the Mafia, or we repeat the names they give themselves, such as the Flaming Eagles (a large, violent Chinese gang) or the Popular Front for the Liberation of Palestine–General Command, but we have at best only the vaguest understanding about how these organizations actually function. But perhaps even more important, we continue to probe and emphasize the significance of the personal histories and perhaps the personal maladjustments of the "bad guy" leaders of such organizations, while at the same time deemphasizing our ignorance about the workings of the organizational structures themselves. A favorite method for covering this ignorance is to refer to some criminal organization by name—for example, the Sendero Luminoso (Shining Path) guerrilla movement of Peru—thereby leaving the impression that we have some degree of understanding regarding its function as an organization. In point of fact, we have very little comprehension about how the group works or how it relates to its complex environment.

The following material presents a case in point. It was taken from a news story about how Chinese gangsters were filling the gap in the heroin supply line left by the U.S. government's prosecution of Mafia drug-traffickers. The news story spells out in some detail the career of one of the Chinese gang leaders, but it provides almost no details about how his gang—the Flaming Eagles—is organized, how it functions, how it relates to the outside noncriminal world, who does what in terms of work roles, or most other facts essential to scientific analysis of this type of criminal organization.

Johnny Kon

During the Vietnam War, Johnny Kon peddled fur coats to American soldiers through their PXs. Later, the Shanghai native arranged R&R tours of Hong Kong for battle-weary GIs. When the war ended, he turned to smuggling furs and selling stolen jewelry.

By 1984, he had gravitated to a more lucrative, and hazardous, business: heroin.

As always, he was in the right place at the right time. The U.S. heroin market, battered by cocaine, was picking up again. Poppy growers in the "Golden Triangle" of Laos, Thailand and Burma (now Myanmar) were producing a more potent heroin that could be smoked rather than injected, cutting the risk of AIDS: meanwhile heroin was proving newly popular to ease the crash after a cocaine high. But thanks to a crackdown on the Mafia, this expanding U.S. heroin market was wide open and promised easy entree for newcomers.

Mr. Kon's response to this opportunity was to form the Flaming Eagles, which would soon become one of the largest and most violent of the Chinese gangs that have rapidly seized control of the U.S. heroin trade. In less than four years, until his 1988 arrest, his organization shipped into the U.S. upward of 1,700 pounds of heroin, with a street value of nearly $1 billion, say agents of the Drug Enforcement Administration. That's enough to supply 1,000 addicts with a daily fix for 30 years.

The story of 46-year-old Johnny Kon, born Kon Yu-Leung and known to accomplices as Big Brother, offers a glimpse into the labyrinthine Chinese underworld that is feeding an ominous surge in U.S. heroin usage. It is a tale of greed, treachery and violence. . . .

As a youth in Shanghai, Mr. Kon says, he joined his uncle's fur-coat factory, training as a tanner and dyer. The Vietnam War broadened his horizons. "In dealing with the Americans, he developed an international outlook," a DEA agent says. "He speaks English, plus Cantonese, Mandarin and Shanghai dialects."

After the war, Mr. Kon exported mink and rabbit coats to the U.S. and Europe through his Hong Kong trading company, Imperial Fur. He also took to smuggling furs to Japan to avoid import taxes.

It wasn't long before he acquired enough status in the underworld to join the Wo Shing Wo triad, one of the Hong Kong groups that deal in drugs, extortion, gambling and other rackets, a DEA agent says. "It was a sign of acceptability," according to the agent. "It opened doors for him." The triads, unlike the Mafia, welcome independent operators. "There was no obligation for Kon to kick money back up the line," the agent says. (Mr. Kon denies belonging to a triad.)

In the early 1980s he began assembling the Flaming Eagles. He signed up several former Chinese "Red Guards" who, after the end of Mao's violent Cultural Revolution, found an outlet for their energies in heroin and armed robbery. "He recruited the best of the worst." . . .

From the recruits, Mr. Kon extracted an oath of silence. "If I betray the oath," each swore, "let the organization deal with me. I will even accept death without complaint."

For a time, the Flaming Eagles robbed Hong Kong jewelry shops and Mr. Kon fenced the booty abroad. When his fur-coat business soured, lawmen say, the allure of heroin proved irresistible. "It was a logical evolution for him," says a DEA agent formerly stationed in Thailand. "The supply side was increasing, and it was easy for him to tap in. He was moving up to make bigger profits with the same amount of risk."

Through his Hong Kong connections, Mr. Kon linked up in 1984 with high-level Chinese heroin brokers in Bangkok. These brokers are supplied by the two outlaw groups that control opium production and refining in the mountainous Golden Triangle: the Shan United Army and the Third Chinese Irregular Force. These renegades, who number in the thousands, move their product by armed caravan into Thailand, where it is readied for shipment to markets overseas.

As it happened, U.S. demand for high-purity Golden Triangle heroin, dubbed "China white," was just then beginning to explode. The abundance of the drug enabled dealers to increase its purity to over 40%, compared with 5% in the past, providing a more intense, addictive high.

Johnny Kon's trafficking career paralleled an abrupt shift in the heroin trade, during which Southeast Asia has overtaken Mexico as America's chief source. Over 40% of heroin in the U.S. now is China white. Opium output in Asia's Golden Triangle has soared fourfold in five years, to 2,400 tons annually, says Andrew J. Maloney, U.S. Attorney in Brooklyn.

During the mid-1980s, federal prosecution of mob leaders in the "Pizza Connection" and "Commission" cases loosened the Sicilian and U.S. Mafia's lock on heroin shipments into New York, the nation's wholesale distribution capital. Chinese gangsters moved in, grabbing 75% to 85% of the New York market, according to Mary Lee Warren of the U.S. Attorney's office in Manhattan. The Mafia now must buy from the Chinese, says Jules J. Bonavolonta, chief of the FBIs organized crime and narcotics division in New York.

Distrusting non-Chinese, the Chinese at first refused to do business with them. This reluctance has broken down in prison, where Asian, white, black and Hispanic heroin dealers have established ties. "Because of these contacts, Chinese traffickers now have a wide distribution network," says Robert M. Stutman, until recently the head of the DEA in New York. (Penn, 1990)

For gaining some understanding of various types of social organizations, both criminal and noncriminal, Cohen (1977)[3] has suggested seven different ways of looking at such structures:

(1) The focus may be on the activity of the members or it may be on the structures of *association* between members. The former stresses social interaction, while the latter focuses on social relationships. Of course, the two are interdependent. To understand one, we must know something about the other.

(2) Criminal organizations frequently require relationships with noncriminal organizations in order to function. A thief may sell his stolen merchandise to a "fence" or to an innocent merchant. *Both* outlets are important for understanding the criminal organization of theft. The thief has the problem of disposing of his stolen goods. For understanding the organization of theft, how the thief solves this problem is part of the description of the organization of his theft. From this perspective, many of those involved with criminal organizations need not themselves be criminal.

(3) With any social organization, a question may be asked regarding its outer limits or boundaries. We may analyze the organization of a butchershop trade on a local, regional, national, or even international basis. In a sense the setting of the boundaries is arbitrary. However, it is important to note that the scope of criminal organization does not embrace that of social organization in general, or that it is indistinguishable from political, economic, ecological and other kinds of organization. Only that which has a *bearing upon criminal action* is to be included within the concept of criminal organization. Many features of banks

are important to depositors and investors. The same features—for example, easy drive-in access to suburban banks—may also be important to bank robbers and, hence, to the analysis of the organization of bank robbery. The difference is analytical rather than concrete or absolute.

(4) The legitimate institutions of government and business do not have to await invasion by alien, criminal intruders, such as drug-traffickers or other organized illegal groups, before becoming corrupted. Legitimate enterprises offer almost unlimited opportunities to be corrupted by insiders. No better example exists of such insider corruption in the 1980s in the United States than the criminal behavior characteristic of the private and governmental groups that participated in one fashion or another in the Iran-Contra Affair. This was not the work of foreign or criminal forces corrupting the executive branch of the U.S. government. The executive branch did this to itself through the illegal behavior of insiders.

(5) Trust in others makes possible the ordinary conduct of social life. Our belief that others are in fact doing what they are supposed to be doing makes family life, work, sports, and other facets of life possible. The same is true of criminal activity. Without the element of trust, organized criminal activity falls apart, or is so overwhelmed with efforts at ensuring trust (security) that enterprises become inefficient and simply disintegrate, sometimes with much violence.

(6) As used here the concept of criminal organization is not limited to organizations with some kind of corporate identity. The idea of criminal organization is meant to apply, on the one hand, to criminal actors who may be individual entrepreneurs, but who also mesh with other criminal actors to form some kind of network of criminal organization. On the other hand, the concept may refer to the large-scale crime syndicate of various times and places. But the concept of criminal organization should not be limited to specific associations whose reason for being is essentially the pursuit of criminal activity. Many different kinds of groups or associations are organized for many different reasons (none of them criminal), and only later may the organizations become involved in criminal activity.

(7) Organizations that generate criminal behavior have the same functional problems as any organization. All organizations are required to cope with problems of resource procurement and allocation, personnel recruitment and socialization, solidarity, legitimacy, discipline, reconciliation of conflicting goals, and so on. Whatever organizations do is to some degree constrained by how they have evolved ways of dealing with such problems. It is possible that some organizations are so rationally organized that all system goals are subservient to the pursuit

of the crime that is the organizations' specialty. On the other hand, other system goals in other criminal organizations may have greater priority than that of crime, such as maintaining "contracts" of trust with competitive criminal organizations to avoid conflict leading to wholesale violence. Many other values may also take priority over an organization's crime goals, such as the need to maintain in-group solidarity or respect for a traditional leader. Thus, many criminal organizations may not have crime as their first priority. Nonetheless, such organizations may over time engage in much criminal activity, while at the same time honoring their more significant goals and values.

The systematic study of multinational criminal organizations would, of course, begin with a review of the related literature. In this fashion, information would be gathered about terrorism or espionage or whatever type of multinational systemic crime was under study. As insights and tentative concepts developed, the more systematic study of such criminal organizations might well begin with an examination of such groups in terms of the above seven perspectives. At the same time additional information from the literature and from primary sources might be developed to expand the data base under analysis. Such a process is likely to yield an increased understanding of how such systems function, in terms of accomplishing their goal of criminal behavior. It is also likely to produce more complete knowledge about the similarities between different types of multinational criminal systems, as well as of the similarities between criminal and noncriminal systems in organizational terms. Such comparisons might do much to enhance an understanding of crime as organizational behavior.

As such an enterprise is undertaken, it would seem perfectly reasonable to assume that:

[I]t is not necessary to invent all our theory as we go along. We will find that there are several bodies of organizational theory, each of which has relevance across a wide range of organizational types. These include general systems theory, structural-functional-theory, and a large, if theoretically somewhat incoherent, sociological literature on formal and informal organizations. These theories may sensitize us to commonalities we have not yet recognized and facets of organization we have not yet explored. (Cohen, 1977)

Since the behavior of some organizations is defined as criminal, this gives to the study of such organizations a certain distinctiveness or emphasis contrasted with the study of noncriminal organizations (Cohen, 1977). One of the main differences is found in the fact that, since criminal behavior is always subject to repression and punishment, secrecy and control over information are crucial for organizational welfare. Yet at the same time, some degree of visibility may be essential to the illegal business at hand—for example, in gambling or prostitution, or in bombings and assassinations for political purposes. In such situations a balance is required between secrecy and publicity. Yet, in other crimes by organizations, maximum secrecy and the control of information are essential features of the activity—for example, in espionage or in state-organized, illegal, clandestine political action. Whatever the situation, secrecy and the control of information are likely to be more central to the functioning of criminal organizations than they are to many noncriminal organizations.

A second problem facing criminal organizations is that of neutralizing law enforcement once information about illegal activity leaks out and becomes known to authorities. There are a variety of devices for doing this, including placating and soothing victims—or threatening and killing victims so that they do not give information to authorities. The same may also be done with witnesses. Law enforcement agents or even total agencies may be corrupted, or police officials, judges, prosecutors, journalists, and others may be selectively assassinated to discourage arrest, prosecution, or extradition. In the extreme, as in Colombia, bombing of public buildings and mass killing may occur to discourage enforcement of the law.

The third problem faced by criminal organizations is the provision of services essential to all organizations, such as access to capital, insurance, banking facilities that are confidential or will accept large amounts of "dirty" money without reporting it to authorities; domestic and international transportation of personnel and cargo; and the hiring and training of new and trustworthy personnel. Methods for solving these problems include paying higher fees for services, or perhaps the criminal organization will start its own bank or, establish its own airline. Or new recruits to terrorist groups may be sent to sympathetic nation-states for training and indoctrination.

A fourth problem is that of maintaining order. There are three facets to this problem. The first is the establishment of a set of rules governing behavior. The second is the assurance of compliance with these rules. The third is the existence of mechanisms for dealing with conflict or rule violations. In both criminal and noncriminal organizations, much of this is accomplished through culture or usage, kinship and friendship, the need for reciprocity, or the force of shame, guilt, or respect. However, when none of these is effective in the noncriminal world and conflict erupts, the state may either be asked to or assert its right to deal with the conflict. In the criminal world this is not usually done. In the criminal world, the parties involved get it resolved on their own. Sometimes this is done through negotiation, mediation, and arbitration, and sometimes through violence. But the significant point is that the state is not utilized to resolve disputes.

A fifth problem, and the final one to be considered, is the problem of legitimacy. Here legitimacy needs to be distinguished from legality. In the strictest sense, the question of legality is settled on the basis of the definitions set down by competent legal authority. But the matter is not that simple. The practitioners of crime might not accept the right of outside authorities to set forth such definitions—for example, in the case of underground resistance to occupation and conquest by foreign powers, or when, on the domestic scene, citizen groups publicly protest state-imposed curfews or bans on public assembly. In such situations, what is technically legal may be lacking in broadly based legitimacy. In this sense of external reference then, the behavior of some organizations may be defined by the state as criminal, but some citizens may disagree and, at one level or another, encourage or even participate in the behavior, claiming exception for various reasons. In terms of internal legitimacy, the problem is that of the criminal organization's justifying to its own members its claims upon them for loyalty, discipline, effort, authority, distribution of rewards, and so forth. The basic question is: How do criminal organizations manage the problem of legitimacy in the eyes of their participants? Some organizations may achieve a measure of acceptance of their criminal

behavior by their participants through "techniques of neutraliza-
tion"; others may do it through socialization in "delinquent subcul-
tures"; or still others may achieve it because of the "focal concerns"
of the social class culture in which their members have been socialized.
But none of this sheds much light on the acceptance as legitimate of
the various internal arrangements characteristic of criminal organizations. The matter of internal legitimacy becomes even more complicated when we consider government organizations, law enforcement
systems, military units, and similar groups. Here members typically
have large investments in public identities and self-conceptions as
patriotic and upright citizens. Yet some, for one reason or another,
find themselves participating in complex criminal conspiracies. How
is this accomplished? How do government officials justify the use of
crime as a means of carrying out the official duties of their office? These
and many other questions bearing on external and internal legitimacy
need to be answered in the study of criminal organizations.

* * *

This ends this chapter's consideration of a perspective for the
study of criminal organizations. It is suggested that the actual application of the perspective to the empirical study of such organizations
is likely to increase our knowledge of the internal workings of such
systems, how they relate to their external environments both criminal
and noncriminal, how such systems relate to each other, and how criminal organizations prosper and under which conditions they decline.

Methodological Orientation of
the Interactionist Perspective[4]

At the core of this perspective is the absolute requirement that
the social scientist must develop an extensive firsthand knowledge
of those areas of social life he wishes to study. The empirical social
world consists of ongoing group life, and one has to get close to this
life to know what is going on in it. There is the need to do a lot of free
exploration in the area to get close to the people involved, seeing and

experiencing the variety of situations they meet, noting their problems and how they solve them, taking part in their conversations, and watching their life as it flows along. Different social groups build up different worlds with different life situations, different beliefs, and different ways of handling their situations. Some examples are military elites, the clergy of a church, big city prostitutes, political insurgents, a gambling syndicate, and so on. Human beings carrying on their collective life form very different kinds of worlds. To study them intelligently one has to know these worlds, and to know them one has to examine them closely and empirically.

Our perception of such worlds takes place on different levels. The social scientist, policy maker, or policeman who perceives such worlds from the outside essentially knows nothing about such worlds and how they work. The person who participates, but is naive and unobservant, will have restricted and inaccurate knowledge. The participant who is very observant and skilled will have fuller and more accurate knowledge, but some levels of happening remain hidden to all participant-observers.

Direct empirical examination of various social worlds is accomplished through two probing, resourceful, flexible, and imaginative methods: exploration and inspection. Exploratory study provides the scholar with an understanding of social life that is unfamiliar to him. Because it is highly flexible and enables the scholar to modify his findings as he progresses, the inquiry, if it is going well, also becomes progressively focused on conceptual tools and relationships. The ultimate aim is to develop as comprehensive and accurate a picture of the area of study as conditions allow.

The descriptive picture unearthed through exploratory research may have considerable value in its own right. However, analysis is also required to specify generic relations, the sharpening of the meaning of concepts, and the formulating of theoretical propositions. This is the proper aim of empirical science, not simply description. Such analysis is accomplished through the inspection of the descriptive picture. As a procedure, inspection consists of examining the different analytical elements involved from a variety of different angles, asking many different questions, and testing out the answers in one way or another. This close, shifting, and analytical scrutiny is the essence of inspection.

Such a direct empirical examination of different social worlds—ranging from a play group to a nation—recognizes social interaction as of vital importance in its own right. Thus:

> Put simply, human beings in interacting with one another have to take account of what each other is going or is about to do; they are forced to direct their own conduct or handle their situations in terms of what they take into account. Thus, the activities of others enter as positive factors in the formation of their own conduct; in the face of the actions of others one may abandon an intention or purpose, revise it, check or suspend it, intensify it, or replace it. The actions of others enter to set what one plans to do, may oppose or prevent such plans, may require a revision of such plans, and may demand a very different set of such plans. One has to *fit* one's own line of activity in some manner to the actions of others. The actions of others have to be taken into account and cannot be regarded a merely an arena for the expression of what one is disposed to do or sets out to do. (Blumer, 1969, p. 8)

In applying the interactionist perspective to the study of a criminal organization, as in the case of a terrorist group, an espionage ring, a cocaine cartel, or some other specific multinational criminal group, the same basic orientation applies, with one modification. In the study of such a large collectivity, the focus is on the directing group or individual who is empowered to assess the operating situation, to note what has to be dealt with, and to map out a line of action. The interaction of such a collectivity takes place in terms of direct orders, discussion, counseling, and debate. Conceptually, the collectivity is in the same position as the individual actor in having to cope with a situation.

* * *

This concludes this chapter's overview of the methodological orientation of the interactionist perspective applied to the study of the internal world of multinational criminal organizations. Obviously, such organizations can usually only be studied one at a time by a single scholar, and access is difficult and often hazardous. Eventually some organizations may prove to be similar to others in various ways. Others may be quite different and even unique. None of this is now very apparent. What the empirical reality turns out to be must await the close and detailed descriptions and analyses by competent observers of such organizations and the ongoing interactions of their key participants.

A Model for Describing Multinational Criminal Organizations and Their Conflict with Other Parties

Social conflict is a relationship between two or more parties who (or whose spokesmen) consciously believe they have incompatible goals. Three different means may be used by the parties to attain their goals: coercion, persuasion, or providing contingent rewards; sometimes different combinations of the three may be used by parties in conflict. Although social conflicts do not necessarily involve coercion and violence, they often do (Kriesberg, 1973, pp. 17-18).

By definition at least two nation-states are involved in multinational systemic crime; the criminal laws of at least one of the nations involved are violated by such crime. Sometimes such criminal violations are committed by the governments of nation-states against other nation-states; sometimes the violations are committed by private organizations against the interests of one or more nations. In the latter case, such criminal organizations may be indirectly protected or covertly sponsored by one or more nation-states, or such organizations may operate without government support.

In studying multinational systemic crime from a conflict perspective, the first task is to identify the parties involved in the conflict. The focus here is on the conflict relationship itself and on the role that particular types of systemic crime play in this relationship. Such crime may be the reason that a conflict relationship develops between parties—for example, smuggling of cocaine into the United States by the Colombian cartels gives rise to the ongoing conflict relationship between the U.S. government and the cartels. On the other hand, multinational crime may be the expression of deeper underlying ongoing conflict between international parties—for example, Israel and the Arab States and the resulting continuing cycle of violence and retaliation ("terrorism") involving both parties.

Once the parties in a particular case have been identified with reasonable certitude, and the role of multinational crime in the conflict relationship between the parties has been specified, the task then, as presented by Louis Kriesberg, becomes one of describing the history and present status of the particular conflict under study in terms of: the five stages of social conflict, "recursions," and spirals.[5]

Through what stages has the conflict under study progressed? What is its present stage? If the struggle has ended, what was the outcome? These and related questions are answered in terms of the following model of a conflict's stages: Social conflicts move through five stages, but not every struggle goes through every stage. Each stage depends upon an earlier one. The *first* or essential stage is the existence of an underlying relationship that is one of social conflict. The *second* emerges when the parties in the relationship either recognize or believe that they have incompatible goals. *Third,* the parties pursue their contradictory goals in some initial way through the use of coercion, persuasion, or rewards. *Fourth,* the intensity and scope of the struggle escalates and de-escalates. *Fifth,* the struggle ends in some way and some outcome occurs. There are four pure types of outcomes: withdrawal, imposition, compromise, and conversion. In an actual outcome to a conflict some combination of these types occurs. Simple imposition of one party's goals over those of an adversary rarely occurs.

What recursions have occurred in the case under study? Recursions refer to the fact that in any conflict later stages may affect earlier ones as the struggle escalates, de-escalates, and otherwise changes. Such backward flow of influence may occur by feedbacks or by anticipation. For example, through feedback, terrorists who experience success in a bombing episode, despite police efforts at prevention before and arrest after the event, may be encouraged to expand their violence to new targets and enter consciously into violent conflict with new adversaries. Anticipation that grossly excessive violence against the police, prosecutors, and judges in the United States may lead to grossly unfavorable outcomes for drug-traffickers may caution traffickers against such escalation.

What has been the history of the case in terms of spirals? Spirals refer to the fact that no conflict leaves the adversaries in exactly the same situation they were in before the struggle began. The outcome of every struggle adds to the information and alters expectations of all parties involved. As long as issues persist, new struggles emerge in modified and different forms based on the experience adversaries have gained from earlier conflicts. The results are cumulative.

The above model by Kriesberg for describing social conflict presumes the rationality of conflict. The parties involved try to calculate costs and benefits, and justify their actions to be consistent with their avowed purposes. Both parties may be misinformed and lack information. Judgments may also be influenced by emotions. *Have the parties involved in the conflict in fact behaved rationally? What part have misinformation, emotion, and so on played?*

The model also presumes that any specific conflict is not purely conflicting. The relationship between parties in a conflict also has cooperative, accommodative, and other qualities. For example, two nation-states actively engaged in espionage and other "cold war" activities against each other for decades may still maintain diplomatic and trade relations with each other. *What have been the nonconflicting aspects of the relationship between the parties?*

Kriesberg's model also cites the importance of interaction between the adversaries. Struggles in all of their phases depend predominantly on the interaction between the conflicting parties. Neither party involved in a conflict can alone determine the course of the conflict; much depends on what the other party does or does not do. Social conflicts also always involve more than the immediate adversaries. All such conflicts occur in a social setting in which other parties are an audience, potential allies of one side or the other, potential beneficiaries if one or the other loses. Such "third parties" watch, wait, and either subtly or blatantly exert their influences on outcomes. *What has been the course and consequences of the interaction between the parties? What have been the roles played by so-called "third parties" to the conflict?*

Finally, in this model for describing social conflicts, there is considerable attention given to the use of noncoercive means in attaining outcomes in conflicts. Persuasion and even rewards may be used to good advantage in achieving outcomes. *What part has been played*

*by the use of noncoercive means in attaining the outcome of the conflict
under study?*

It is not desirable to close this discussion of multinational systemic
crime as perceived from a social conflict perspective without considering the "settings" in which such conflicts occur. Such conflicts are
international, sometimes global, within a world that is poorly integrated politically. There is also little by way of institutionalized decision-
making structures at the global level. Governments presume sovereignty and help one another in supporting this principle. But perhaps
one of the most outstanding characteristics of today's world remains
the highly diverse and fundamentally different social and cultural systems characterizing the different regions, nations, and subnational
areas that become involved in international conflicts. In particular
conflicts related to multinational crime, such social and cultural systems
merit extensive study in their own right. They constitute only one com-
ponent of the total international setting within which multinational
crime occurs. Yet an understanding of them is usually crucial in com-
prehending the course of social conflict as it relates to multinational
crime. In the next chapter descriptions are provided for three such regions: the Golden Triangle of Southeast Asia; the Andean region of Colombia, Bolivia, and Peru; and the Middle East.

Finally, as Kriesberg concludes, as a general principle it is wise for
one adversary to take the role of the other as a struggle develops. This
is a limited application of the interactionist perspective described at
length earlier in this chapter. The ability of each party to view a conflict
from its adversary's perspective does much to decrease the possibility of mistakes and disasters. *In the case of a particular conflict being
examined, does it appear that one or both parties were able to take the
role of the other? What are the consequences of the success or failure
of such interaction?*

A Note on the Sources of Data

In studying criminal organizations, in applying the interactionist
perspective to such organizations, and in applying a conflict model
to multinational crime, there are no strict rules, procedures, or limitations.
Within ethical limits the only rule is to get results measured in terms

of the empirical data required. Direct observation, the use of life histories and biographies, letters and diaries, newspaper reports and feature articles, participant observation, public documents, the use of conversations, and group discussions are all important data sources. Of special importance is the identification of key participants in the area of life under study who are articulate, well informed, and respected among their peers. Such individuals, either alone or in small informal groups, may not only be able to provide significant amounts of information and interpretations about the object of the study, but may also be able to safely introduce the outside scholar into the area of social life he is investigating. Obviously, such introductions may be invaluable. The literature of social science bears witness to the fact that when well-trained and talented investigators use such sources as those cited above, they have produced many successful, even classic, studies.[6]

NOTES

1. In this regard it is interesting to note that in 1989 *Forbes* magazine listed Pablo Escobar Gaviria of Colombia, who is head of the Medellín cocaine cartel, among the top 25 billionaires in the world. Nine on the list were Japanese, seven were European, four were American, three were Canadian, one was Korean. Only Escobar Gaviria was from Latin America. See Phillips (1990, p. 119).

2. For a description of regional political power in Southeast Asia based on opium, see Posner (1988).

3. This and subsequent references to Cohen are adapted from his article as cited. In the process, language and examples have been modified, but every effort has been made not to alter meaning.

4. This section is adapted from Blumer (1969).

5. This and the following sections about social conflict are adapted from Kriesberg (1973).

6. Only a few such studies will be noted here for purposes of reference. Some of these also include extensive descriptions of the methodologies used by their authors: Ianni & Reuss-Ianni (1972); Klockars (1974); Liebow (1967); Lifton (1986); Posner (1988); Prange, Goldstein, & Dillon (1984); Sutherland (1937); Thrasher (1927); Wakefield (1959); Whyte (1955).

6

Some Historical and Contemporary Contexts of Multinational Systemic Crime

The proper study of multinational systemic crime appears to require a sound understanding of the historical and contemporary environmental contexts from which such systems emerge and within which they act. The assumption is that the social, cultural, economic, and political content of such contexts has been instrumental in promoting the emergence, growth, behavior, and social character of the particular criminal organizations identified for study. It needs to be clearly understood, however, that the three regional Third World contexts of multinational crime described in this chapter provide only a partial and limited description of the full range of regions involved in multinational crime globally. Moreover, and most important, descriptions of the environmental contexts out of which multinational criminal organizations emerge and function yield only partial understanding of the complex social conflict between such organizations and other parties involved in the interaction. For example, understanding the Middle East yields little understanding of what role the United States has played in attracting the Middle Eastern terrorism directed against it. Nevertheless, the three descriptions do provide an important understanding of the regional contexts from which some of the criminal organizations involved in today's multinational crime emerge and function. If Western nations wish to control multinational crime emanating from these three regional sources, then the West might do well to plan such strategies with a full comprehension and awareness of the history, present character, limits, and excesses of the regions, their rulers, and their people.

The study of crime in terms of the environmental contexts in which it occurs has a long tradition in criminology. Since the early nineteenth century, for example, hundreds of studies have sought to relate crime rates to changes in the levels of poverty, unemployment, the price of rye, and other economic conditions.

Considerable attention has also been given in a variety of studies of "high crime areas" in cities through the application of what became known as the "theory of human ecology." This viewed a city as a sort of ever-changing social organism with "natural areas" constantly being impacted by the change process of invasion, dominance, and succession by immigrant and other social groups and land-use patterns. In the so-called high crime areas, change was closely related to lowered economic status, increases in cases of tuberculosis, increases in chronic "social disorganization," and increases in crime and delinquency.

This same general perspective has also been offered to explain why regions or culture areas are important for understanding the distribution of crime either within a nation or between various nations. Thus, the murder rate in the southern United States is much higher than in New England. However, the murder rate in the United States as a whole is consistently higher than in most European countries, but lower than in most Latin American countries. These differences are generally explained in terms of structural differences and the "subculture of violence."

Although many valid criticisms have been made of the various studies and theories that have represented this environmental tradition in the history of criminology, the general perspective has become widely established and accepted in the field. It is the application of this perspective to the description and analysis of the varied international environments, in which different multinational criminal organizations arise and act, that holds much promise for the successful study of such groups and their illegal behavior. The great difficulty, of course, is that such criminal organizations often arise and operate out of such diverse foreign regions, frequently situated in distant parts of the Third World, that access to relevant environmental data is complicated. Fortunately, the available literature appears to contain considerable material most useful for understanding something about the regions from which some multinational criminal organizations emerge.

Three illustrations from this literature are presented below. The *first* describes the ecological and political environments of the Golden Triangle of Southeast Asia that make the area so ideal not only for the production of opium but also for the development of criminal organizations that traffic in drugs. The *second* describes the present economic and political strengths of the cocaine industry in Colombia, Bolivia, and Peru—the major sources of cocaine. It also considers the enormous difficulty of controlling the production and exportation of cocaine, given its importance to the Andean economy and the political power of both organized coca farmers and the separate but related trafficking syndicates in the area. The *third* is a brief statement about the history, culture, and politics of the Middle East, which is instructive for an understanding of what the United States and some other nations have called "organized terrorism" in the area.

NARCOTICS IN THE GOLDEN TRIANGLE

This material describes the political economy of Southeast Asia's Golden Triangle, where opium production and narcotics refining and trafficking have long presented a major problem. A complex of factors has come together to make the region one of the world's key sources of narcotics. Despite the application of control strategies over the years by both the United States and governments in the area, the opium economy of the area continues to thrive. The region may be characterized as follows:

The Ecological Environment

The Geographical Setting. The geography of the Golden Triangle provides the essential environment for a thriving opium economy. On one hand, the topographical and climatic conditions are ideal for the cultivation of opium, and the demographic characteristics of the region ensure the kind of division of labor necessary to sustain a widespread economic system rooted in opium cultivation, narcotics refining and trafficking. On the other hand, these conditions all mitigate against the extension of the control measures which would enforce the laws against opium cultivation, or the development initiatives which might offer an alternative to opium culture.

Topography has been a key factor in the development of the opium economy. The Golden Triangle, an area of perhaps 150,000 square miles, extends from Burma's Chin Hills in the west, north into China's Yunnan Province, east into Laos and Thailand's northwestern provinces, and south into Burma's Kayah State. It encompasses all of the Shan State of Burma, the principal battleground in today's narcotics wars. Although often referred to as the "Shan Plateau," the region is largely mountainous, characterized by range after range of steep mountains running generally north to south. Elevations range from 1,500 meters to more than 3,000 meters. Historically, settlement and development in the Golden Triangle have followed the river valleys, parts of four major river systems. In the north, the NaMali and Shweli, tributaries of Burma's great Irrawaddy River, flow out of Yunnan's mountains through deep gorges in the northern Shan State and Kachin State. To the south, the Shan Plateau is cut on the west by the Sittang River and to the east by the Salween, the principal arterial route of the Shan State. Farther east, the Mekong River spills out of southern China and flows south and east, cutting the eastern Shan Plateau and providing a natural boundary between Burma and Laos, and Laos and Thailand.

While these great rivers and their tributaries have provided the traditional lines of communication, the principal routes along which migration and trade took place, in the twentieth century they have been major obstacles to the political integration of Burma. Whether in Pagan one thousand years ago or in Rangoon today, the historical problem for Burma's rulers has been how to extend the writ of the capital east to the Shan Plateau when there are no natural routes along which this power can be projected. Today, only two major roads extend into the Shan State from Burma's Irrawaddy heartland—the old Burma road which runs from Mandalay north through Lashio to the China border (a rail line runs parallel to the road until Lashio), and the Mandalay to Tachilek road which connects Burma to northwestern Thailand. Though nominally macadam, all-weather roads, both are in relatively poor shape and subject to periodic closure or interruption by washouts, bridge collapses and land slides. Banditry has long plagued the routes, making all but convoy travel risky. The absence of services along the way has contributed further to travel problems. While these routes have facilitated the extension of Burmese control in contiguous areas, elsewhere the government has had to rely on either air routes or, along with most of the inhabitants of the Golden

Triangle, on foot or animal travel. Air transportation has been seriously constrained by the limited number of airports and its great cost.

In these geographical circumstances, the Burmese government has lacked the resources necessary to overcome the physical obstacles to greater political integration. In its absence, politics has been dominated both by attempts to foster greater disintegration (e.g., Shan separatism) and by efforts to capitalize on the economic opportunities created by such anarchy. To these ends, the complex ethnographic landscape has provided a fertile ground for both the politics of disintegration and the political economy of opium.

The Ethnographic Landscape. An anthropologist might describe the ethnography of the Golden Triangle as complex-complex. The region is inhabited by a multitude of ethnic groups. Simple ethnic classifications—Burman, Shan, Kachin, Thai, Yunnanese—are only marginally useful in understanding the ethnic diversity of the region. These labels mask complex differences within each group—for instance, Kachin or Jinghphaw have at least 25 different, and mutually unintelligible dialects, while the Shan vary widely in their culture across the Shan Plateau.

What complicates our understanding of the ethnography (and even more so the politics) of the Golden Triangle is the presence of numerous other groups which are not part of the larger ethnic divisions. These include the Ahka, Hong, Lisu, Lahu, Karenni, Padaung, Pa-O, Palaung, and Wa, to name the major groups. With the Shan and Kachin, they make up about 20 percent of Burma's population. None of these ethnic groups, however, are geographically localized, but rather they are scattered throughout the region horizontally and vertically—their settlement varies not only with latitude but also with elevation. Burman and Shan tend to dwell in the river valleys in settled areas while the smaller minorities are largely mountain dwellers whose slash-and-burn agricultural practices necessitate frequent moves. Political boundaries, imposed during the period of colonization, were drawn with little regard to ethnicity. Few of the ethnic groups are sufficiently localized to provide the ethnic foundations for territorial political organization; at the same time, state boundaries and national borders have frequently cleaved ethnic groups. All of these minorities have sought in one fashion or another to maintain their separate identities, often militantly, making insurgency the dominant form of politics in the region. This has not only presented serious challenges to the central governments but, given the inherent irredentism of the groups, has also provided an endless series of irritants in relations between states in the Golden Triangle.

In the post-World War II period, this "bias towards the periphery" has been greatly exacerbated by the development of the Golden Triangle narcotics business. Opium production and narcotics trafficking have percolated through all aspects of the Triangle's politics. Insurgencies have been fueled by the funds derived from the opium economy while narcotics traffickers have increasingly taken on the form and style of insurgents. Aspects of narcotics control have inescapably become embedded in counter- insurgency strategies and vice-versa. Before looking at the political structure of the Golden Triangle, however, it is necessary to have some appreciation of opium cultivation and the production of narcotics.

Opium Agriculture. The Golden Triangle has provided ideal conditions for opium cultivation—excellent climatic and soil conditions, abundant, cheap labor for the labor-intensive growing period, and a ready market for its traditional derivatives. Opium appears to have been introduced into Burma's highlands from the Near East around the sixteenth-seventeenth century, and many of Burma's mountain-dwelling minorities took up limited cultivation and consumption of opium. Opium, which may be eaten, smoked, or drunk in potions, was absorbed into local culture for both medicinal reasons and recreational purposes. At the same time, its cultivation complemented the traditional slash-and-burn agriculture practiced by the hill tribes.

The opium growing season generally runs from September to March while upland rice and maize crops can be planted after opium is harvested, thus providing the cultivator with the opportunity to grow both food and cash crops in the same area.

While early cultivation seems to have been largely for local consumption, the growth of urban Chinese communities with addict populations provided an expanded market—opium was introduced to China in the seventeenth century and the migration of Chinese laborers to Southeast Asia greatly stimulated the growth in addiction in Burma and Thailand. By the twentieth century opium had become a popular cash crop in the frontier areas and a division of labor developed within the Golden Triangle linking small cultivators with urban markets through brokers and traders.

Until World War II the opium economy rested largely on raw and cooked opium sales. Heroin, the crystalline hydrochloride precipitated from opium, did not become a major factor in the economy until after World War II with the growth of Chinese addiction to smoking heroin.

This change brought the first internationalization of the Golden Triangle trade, as syndicates developed to move smoking heroin to Hong Kong and Chinese communities in Europe. The Vietnam War, however, brought the major stimulus to change, and it was to meet the market presented by U.S. troops in Indochina that the opium economy under-went fundamental structural change and became as much a heroin economy.

Opium Production. At present, there are major concentrations of opium cultivation in the following areas:

1. Burma: Throughout the Shan State particularly heavy cultivation exists in the old Kokang and Wa States and in eastern and southeastern Shan State in the area running southwest from Kengtung to Kayah State. Some cultivation has taken place in the Tiddim and Falam areas of Chin State, but this has probably been for local consumption.
2. Thailand: Cultivation is concentrated in the mountainous areas of Chiang Mai and Chiang Rai Provinces, with some scattered growth in Mae Hong Son and Nan Provinces.
3. Laos: Data is limited, but incidental reporting suggests heaviest growth is in Houakhong, Hongsa, and Louangprabang Provinces.
4. China: There is some government-controlled opium cultivation—in the 1970s estimated at 100 tons—in Southwest China. Given the heavy culti-vation on the Burmese side of the Sino-Burma border, there is undoubt-edly illicit cultivation in the tribal areas of Yunnan Province. . . .

The Political Environment

In order to understand the Golden Triangle political economy and the insurgency and instability that plague the Shan plateau today, it is nec-essary to have some appreciation for the different groups which are parties to the conflict. As with everything else in the region, the task is easier stated than done. Simply ethnic or political taxonomies are inad-equate because few of the groups fit neatly into any categories. For instance, not all groups which call themselves Shan are Shan; similarly, ideological affiliations may mask contradictory economic ties—the opium business provides stranger bedfellows than politics; and polit-ical programs may be less (or more) than they seem. These caveats aside, several different groups or parties to the conflict will be briefly examined:

1. Ethnic insurgents: If a group can be defined as ethnically distinct either from Burmans or from other ethnic groups, it will probably have some insurgent form seeking either independence or greater autonomy from Rangoon. While goals are nominally political, most of the ethnically based groups in the Shan Plateau have made their accommodations with the narcotics business.
2. Revolutionary movements: These groups are distinguished from the ethnic insurgents more by their goals than their composition. Such groups are seeking to overthrow the central government and replace it with their own political organization rather than separate from the central govern-

ment. Here, we will be primarily concerned with the Burmese Communist movement.

3. Warlord organizations: Whereas the first two groups are essentially concerned with either seizing power in Rangoon, or controlling some specific territory to create an autonomous state, warlord groups are preoccupied with illicit market activities—narcotics production and trafficking loom largest—and controlling illicit trade routes.

4. Syndicates and consortia: While some warlord organizations, particularly the Shan United Army, directly control refineries, many heroin laboratories are owned by syndicates of traffickers. Either operating as a trading company or as a consortia of traffickers owning shares in a refinery, they finance the purchase of opium, the cost of transport and protections, and the operation of the refinery including the provision of precursor chemicals. Politically well connected, they can protect the refineries from police raids and frustrate narcotics control activity. It is through these syndicates that the refined heroin moves into the international trafficking system.

The Ethnic Insurgents: The Shan insurgency, the movement that has sought to realize Shan aspirations for an identity separate from Burman or Burmese through either federation or separatism, can be traced directly back to the government's decision in 1958 not to recognize the Shan leaders' right to succession conferred on them by the 1947 Panglong Agreements.

Although the facts of this 1958 decision have long since been lost in both Shan and government propaganda, it is important to remember that the majority of Shan leaders agreed to sell their feudal rights to the government, and that there was an emerging new Shan elite which was trying to carve out a place for itself in modern Burmese politics. There was an incipient movement of reactionary Shan leaders coalescing around the Mahadevi of Yaunghwe, wife of Sao Shwe Thaike, Burma's first president, which threatened succession, but there was also the younger Shan leaders of the Shan State People's Freedom League (SSPFL) who had allied themselves with the Burman socialist leaders.

The 1962 coup by the Burmese military and the radical, revolutionary program of socialist unity which it ushered in propelled the reactionary group into active insurgency. The SSPFL, on the other hand, was torn apart by the coup. The SSPFL leader, U Tun Aye, joined forces with the military government, and became the ranking Shan member of the new Burma Socialist Program Party and chairman of the new Revolutionary Government's Shan State Affairs Council. Some of his Shan colleagues joined him, others moved under the umbrella of the Mahadevi, and some set about to fashion a separate Shan movement, one neither reactionary nor collaborative. These choices did not exhaust the possibilities. The difficulty for the Shan insurgent leaders was that there were so many possibilities and that there was so little common agreement on either goals or organization. In the absence of common purpose, alliances among Shan were always fragile and the Shan movement remained fragmented, a victim of the fissiparous tendencies of its leaders. For Shan leaders with aspirations for greater power, this inability to forge a unified movement among the Shan meant going beyond the Shan community for allies, whether they were other ethnic insurgents, warlord organizations, or other groups—remnants of Nationalist Chinese troops (Kuomintang or KMT), Taiwanese para-military teams, or corrupt Thai, for example. Alliances transcended ethnicity, regionalism, ideology, and economics, but over the long run alliances with non-Shan proved as fragile and transitory as those with Shan. Today the principal Shan insurgent organization is the Shan State Progress Party (SSPP) and its military arm, the Shan State Army (SSA). This movement, which is going through one of its periodic hard times, can trace its lineage back to the early days of Shan separatism, but the lines are convoluted. The movement has grown through myriad permutations and alliances with other insurgent or narcotics trafficking organizations.

Other Shan State Ethnic Insurgents: Although historically the Shan have dominated the Shan plateau through their political organization, the region is inhabited by a multitude of minorities. Some, like the Pa-O, are ethnically close to the Shan; others, such as the Lahu, Lisu, and Akha, share only geography in common with the Shan. All, at one time or another, have had some armed form of insurgency. . . .

Revolutionary Organizations: Though the Burmese Communist Party (BCP) is one of Burma's oldest insurgent groups—underground since 1948—it did not become a significant factor in the Shan State insurgencies until 1967, when the Chinese-backed insurgents opened a second front in the northern Shan State in the area east of the Salween River. The BCP's military force, estimated at 8,000-15,000, drew heavily on Ahka, Lisu, Lahu, and Wa minorities for recruitment. It also appealed to the more organized insurgent forces to form alliances, and some Kachin and Shan insurgents have periodically allied with the BCP.

After the tension of the Cultural Revolution, there has been a gradual improvement in relations between Rangoon and Beijing. This has apparently resulted in a substantial reduction of Chinese material support to the BCP, and by the 1980s there were signs that aid levels had dropped sharply. This had two consequences for the BCP's relations with other Shan insurgent groups. First, it reduced the material advantages which the BCP had enjoyed. The Communists' ability to provide weapons and ammunition to its alliance partners was central to many of these alliances. Without these material incentives, other insurgent leaders had less reason to make common cause with the BCP. Ideological bonds between the BCP and their Shan or other ethnic allies were not terribly strong —discontent with Rangoon was their strongest tie to each other—and although some factions of the Shan State Army were ideologically disposed to the BCP, the reduction in material aid cut to the heart of BCP alliances. The most notable split with the BCP at this time was the 1979 decision by the first Battalion of the Shan State Army (sometimes referred to as the Shan State Army-North) to break with the BCP and return to cooperation with the mainstream of the Shan State Army. A Lahu insurgent organization, the A Bi group, also split with the BCP's Northeast Command around this time. This group, however, retains its Communist identification. The second consequence of the altered Chinese-BCP relationship was the apparent decision of the BCP to move deeply into the opium economy as an alternative means to support its insurgent activity. BCP forces operate in areas that account for nearly half of Burma's opium production. While local BCP leaders had probably been involved in brokering opium sales to some of the warlord organizations, the BCP Central Committee had publicly opposed opium cultivation and narcotics trafficking. Since 1979 there have been increasing signs that the BCP leadership has sanctioned opium sales and that the BCP has developed its own narcotics production and sales capability. Details of this activity are sketchy, but as a result of earlier alliances it appears that there are senior BCP leaders with deep experience in the opium trade. One of the key BCP military commanders, Peng Chi'a-fa, was at one time a key lieutenant of Lo Hsinghan. He is in a position to develop BCP narcotics production and sales, particularly in the Kokang and northern Wa State area.

During the summer of 1980 Rangoon began secret negotiations with the BCP, which had been encouraged by the Chinese to arrive at some accommodation with the Burmese government. In July 1981, Burmese President Ne Win announced the failure of these talks. Collapse of the negotiations undercut Rangoon's efforts to bring some sense of normalcy to the northern Shan Plateau. Had Ne Win been successful, he would then have been able to concentrate his efforts against the other Shan State insurgencies and warlord groups. Since the failed negotiations the BCP has resumed military action, albeit not on the scale of the late 1970s. It has also sought to expand its tie with other insurgent and narcotics trafficking organizations.

According to press reports, the BCP has renewed links to the Lahu A Bi organization giving the BCP access to the narcotics market on the Thai-Burma border. At the same time, there are indications that the BCP is dealing with the Shan United Army with the SUA providing weapons for the BCP in return for opium from BCP controlled areas. The BCP also seems to have resurrected its alliance with some elements of the Shan State Army. The significance of these ties for the BCP is uncertain, but the decision on the part of the SSA leaders appears to have rent that organization's command once again. On June 21, 1983, Sao Hso Lane, leader of the Shan State Army and a long time stalwart of the Shan insurgency, rallied to the government. He had broken with the Shan State Progress Party over the decision to renew links to the BCP.

Warlord Organizations: Warlord organizations are an artifact of the historical development of the Golden Triangle and have probably existed in the northern and eastern Shan State since the eighteenth century. Led by ethnic Chinese—Han or Yunnanese—or Sino-Shan, they have sought to control trade between "kingdoms" and have built armed organizations to protect their caravans and operational bases. Most established alliances with the local Shan leaders.

During the Sino-Japanese War and World War II many of these groups were mobilized into the Kuomintang Army in northern Burma. After the war, some remained as KMT units fighting the Chinese Communists, while others returned to their trading-smuggling activities, frequently in alliance with Shan State political leaders.

In 1967, confronted with a Chinese-backed Burmese Communist insurgency, Rangoon deputized 50 of these warlord armies as mobile militias. Called Ka Kwei Yei (KKY), they were given patents by the central government to engage in smuggling, including opium, in return for their commitment to fight Burmese Communist insurgents. In 1971-1973, Rangoon outlawed the KKY. Some returned to the government fold, while others moved deeply into narcotics trafficking, a thriving industry as the war escalated in Vietnam. . . . (Waint, 1985)

COCAINE, ECONOMICS, AND POLITICAL POWER

Coca-growing and cocaine-trafficking in the Andean region of South America also take place in a enormously complicated environmental context. It is impossible to comprehend the economic and political characteristics of the area without considering the great influence of the highly organized cocaine interests. The following description addresses these facts.

Supply side approaches . . . have obviously failed to stem the flow of cocaine into U.S. markets. Latin American governments lack the resources to counter the traffic: There is no correspondence between the resources available to cocaine traffickers and the resources available to combat them. Perhaps more important, however, governments and important constituencies in the main producing countries do not give the war against cocaine their unconditional support. This is true even though the cocaine traffic in many respects damages the source countries—rampant corruption, rising numbers of drug addicts, escalating levels of violence, declining moral standards, and a deteriorating national image are among the more obvious consequences. The reasons for this Latin American reticence are complex. . . .

First, moving against the cocaine traffic entails serious economic and political costs. Narco-dollars have represented a relatively important source of foreign exchange for Andean countries, as traditional sources—foreign investment, bank loans, and earnings from Andean exports such as oil, gas, copper, and fishmeal—have contracted. The cocaine industry is an important source of jobs and income in regions characterized by desperate poverty and widespread unemployment. An estimated 500,000 to one million people are employed directly in the upstream and downstream phases of the industry—cultivation, initial processing, refining, and smuggling. Coca farmers receive less than one percent of the final street value of their crop—that is, the equivalent value of refined cocaine sold to consumers in industrialized countries—yet, they typically earn several times the income they would receive from growing alternative crops such as cacao, oranges, and coffee. All along the cocaine production-logistics chain, people receive substantially higher wages than they would in the licit economy. Second, the cocaine industry as a whole has accumulated significant political clout. Coca farmers are numerous and well organized; in Bolivia, national labor and campesino organizations provide direct political support to farmers. Cocaine traffickers play the role of power brokers and are a major source of funding for political campaigns. Traffickers also have penetrated and corrupted nearly every important national institution: police forces, military establishments, legislatures, key government ministries, the judiciary, the church, and the news media. Some cocaine traffickers exhibit a rudimentary sense of social responsibility—a critically important development that enabled them to build a popular following by sponsoring public works and welfare projects that benefit the urban and rural poor.

Third, the war on cocaine is not especially popular in South America—it is perceived as a program imposed on South America by the United States. Certain U.S.-initiated measures—such as extradition, the spraying of illicit crops, U.S. military intervention against cocaine laboratories, and economic sanctions against cocaine-exporting countries—have provoked considerable anti-Yankee sentiment. Furthermore, most Latin American leaders see the supply-side approach to drug control as fundamentally flawed: In the Latin American view, demand, not supply, drives the international drug traffic. Says Peru's Allan Garcia: "I have always thought of drug trafficking as the final stage of capitalist consumerism. The problem does not lie in the fact that a poor town produces coca leaves in the Peruvian jungle. The basic problem lies in the world's big consumer markets consisting of the richest societies."

This is not to say that the drug war in South America is totally useless. It at least limits the inroads that traffickers can make into the political system. Today, it is significantly harder than it was in the early 1980s for cocaine dealers to run for political office, to form "nationalist" political parties, and to occupy cabinet-level positions. Yet, limiting the more outrageous political manifestations of the cocaine trade is not the same as curbing exports of cocaine from South America. On this count, U.S. programs and those of the Andean countries themselves have largely failed. This was not written as a polemic against supply-side approaches to drug control. However, research and interviews . . . and subsequent analyses lead inevitably to several conclusions that advocates of supply-side programs will find discouraging. First, the cocaine trade has altered irrevocably the economic and political landscape of the Andean countries. Cocaine traffickers constitute an interest group with extensive resources and political connections, just like the coffee barons in Colombia or the mining elites in Peru and Bolivia. Indeed, studies of these countries' development patterns, decision making processes, and relations with other countries are no longer possible without reference to coca and cocaine.

Second, the drug war in South American source countries presents difficult if not unmanageable problems for both South American governments and the U.S. government. The drug war requires that Andean countries address a host of obstacles, such as national economic dependence on drugs, powerful narcotics lobbies, indifferent or hostile publics, weak political structures, and porous systems of criminal justice. In addition, other compelling U.S. interests in the regions—such as promoting economic stability, preserving democracy, or preventing the emergence of Marxist regimes—are not necessarily compatible with aggressive drug control programs.

Third, even with significant U.S. help, Andean governments will make little progress in controlling cocaine production. Eradication campaigns, occasional large drug busts, and a few major arrests (like the highly publicized arrests of Carlos Lehder in Colombia and Roberto Suarez in Bolivia) will continue in the Andean countries. Nonetheless, the basic structure of the cocaine industry—its agricultural base, manufacturing infrastructure, leadership, smuggling networks, and so on—will remain more or less intact. . . .

The Cocaine Trade and South American Economies

Colombia, Bolivia, and Peru are all, to a greater or lesser extent, economically dependent on the cocaine industry. The industry is not by any means the most effective source of revenue for the economies of these nations; in fact, the wealth that it generates is not converted very efficiently into economic growth and may even retard growth in certain areas. The majority of narco-dollars are probably banked or invested abroad, and traffickers' domestic spending priorities certainly do not coincide with those of national economic planners (core economic activities seem to be shortchanged). A recent article in *The Economist* reported, "The economic impact of $4 billion spent bribing politicians and buying status symbols will usually be less than that of $1 billion spent building roads and electricity generators."

Yet, cocaine earnings clearly add to a country's foreign exchange reserves, and cocaine production obviously constitutes a significant source of employment. The industry apparently has transformed the economic life of specific localities and communities that either are centers of illicit drug cultivation or are near such centers. Perhaps most important, the cocaine traffic may serve as a safety valve of sorts for countries or regions experiencing economic decline or stagnation. For example, according to a Bolivian government document, "Triennial Program for the Battle Against Drug Trafficking," Bolivia's gross national product declined by 2.3 percent per year from 1980 to 1986, but coca production annually grew an estimated 35 percent during those years. The official unemployment rate more than tripled from 1980 to 1986 (from 5.7 percent to 20 percent), but so did the number of families reportedly growing coca. During 1986, more than 20,000 Bolivian miners lost their jobs, and as many as 5,000 may have sought work in the coca fields. Cocaine exports can compensate for the loss of foreign exchange from traditional sources, a phenomenon illustrated from 1983 to 1987, when Bolivia's exports shrank by 39 percent and Peru's by 15 percent, primarily because world prices for traditional Andean commodities—oil, natural gas, and tin—declined precipitously during the same period. As the head of Peru's Investigative Commission on Narcotics remarked in a 1986 interview, "The price of copper goes down, the price of oil goes down, the price of oil products for export goes down, and the only price that increases is that of cocaine."

In Colombia, the rise of the cocaine industry paralleled and partly compensated for the decline of Medellín in the 1970s as a major industrial center. Medellín's leading industrial sector, textiles, nearly collapsed because of Asian competition and punitive import tariffs. The depression lingered into the 1980s: From 1980 to 1985, the unemployment rate in Medellín was consistently higher than that of the other three major cities

(Cali, Bogotá, and Barranquilla). In 1986, only Barranquilla suffered from a higher unemployment rate. Consequently, many Medellín residents were drawn into the cocaine traffic: "Owners of small or middle-sized companies that were bankrupt or on the verge of bankruptcy, unemployed professionals, housewives who had no income, and other unemployed persons, skilled and unskilled." The Colombian economist Mario Arango estimates that approximately 60 billion pesos ($313 million) of proceeds from illegal exports—mostly cocaine exports—flowed into Medellín's economy in 1987, producing local inflationary effects, but also stimulating a mini-boom in textiles, construction, and other industries. As a result, 28,000 new jobs were created in Medellín that year. From 1983 to 1987, Medellín's unemployment rate as a percent of the national rate dropped from 140 percent to 98 percent.

If the cocaine industry does not operate as an efficient engine of economic progress, it still provides an escape from abject poverty and misery for many inhabitants of the Andean world. Moreover, for rural dwellers especially, the cocaine industry offers a kind of instant introduction to modern life styles—the chance to enjoy color television, videocassette recorders, high-tech sound systems, and the latest-model Toyota landcruiser or Datsun car. Consequently, coca cultivation and cocaine trafficking have created radically new expectations and aspirations within Andean societies. If revolutions truly are born of frustrated expectations, the prospect of the sudden destruction or collapse of the cocaine industry should give nightmares to South American leaders— and to leaders in Washington as well.

The Politics of Cocaine

The Coca Lobby

The cocaine industry also has amassed significant political clout in the Andean countries because of the industry's large popular base in the upstream phases growing and harvesting coca leaves and its enormous financial aid logistical capabilities in the downstream phases processing, refining, and smuggling cocaine. Farmers who cultivate illicit cocathe most visible cocaine constituency—are highly organized, sometimes well-armed, and capable of exerting tremendous pressure on governments.

In Peru's Upper Huallaga Valley, where more than 90 percent of farm income stems from coca cultivation, coca farmers are represented by provincial and district self-defense fronts (FEDIPs). FEDIPs are heavily influenced by the political left (the Izquierda Unida) and also receive support from the Sendero Luminoso (Shining Path) and Tupac Amaru guerrilla movements. FEDIPs lobby for the legalization of coca cultivation and chal-lenge government eradication teams with strikes, roadblocks, and other forms of mass violence. Because of coca growers' opposition and security problems, a U.S.-Peruvian eradication project in the Valley ground to a virtual halt in 1987. That year, only 355 hectares were destroyed, compared to 2,575 in 1986 and 4,830 in 1985. In 1988, the total increased to 5,130 hectares, primarily because eradication teams cut down coca bushes instead of uprooting them. The trouble with cutting down plants is that they grow back and can be in full production in 18 months. Unless Peru can proceed with a serial spraying program—and to date there is no demonstrably safe and effective herbicide against coca—control of coca cultivation in the Upper Huallaga is most likely a lost cause.

In Bolivia, the dynamics look even worse: an estimated 70,000 coca-growing families (organized in 10 regional federations in the Yungas and the Chapare) receive direct political support from national mass membership organizations—the 1.3-million member Bolivian Workers Congress and its main affiliate, the Confederation of Bolivian Peasant Workers. In a country of only 6.4 million people, such support constitutes a significant deterrent to narcotics control programs. U.S.-Bolivian attempts to pressure coca farmers by destroying crops or by regulating the sale of coca leaves trigger organized resistance on a national scale. The Bolivian coca lobby has the power to shut down parts of Bolivia's fragile transportation system. For example, coca farmers and their worker-peasant allies have sealed off Cochabamba, Bolivia's third largest city, four times since 1983 to protest several anti-coca policies of the Bolivian government. Bolivia did eradicate slightly more than 1,000 hectares of coca in 1987, but only by undertaking a complex process of bargaining with federations and individual syndicates and by paying peasants $2,000 for each hectare eradicated. Involuntary eradication on any significant scale is probably a political impossibility in Bolivia.

Trafficking Syndicates

The criminal syndicates that refine, smuggle, and distribute cocaine are equally important in the political scheme of things and overwhelmingly important in Colombia. The South American cocaine trade displays varying degrees of concentration. For example, five loosely organized syndicates headquartered in Medellín and Cali control an estimated 70-80 percent of the cocaine exported from Colombia and about 60-70 percent of all cocaine sold in the United States. Bolivia's cocaine trade is controlled by some 12 to 25 families; most of them run cattle ranches or commercial farms in the Beni, Cochabamba, and Santa Cruz regions. In Peru, on the other hand, the industry is highly fragmented and is organized and, to a large extent, dominated by Colombian traffickers.

Colombia is clearly the linchpin—the *pais clave*—of the South American cocaine industry. the Medellín-Cali syndicates procure raw materials in Peru and Bolivia, manufacture refined cocaine in Colombia, ship cocaine in large loads of 300 kilograms (kilos) or more to the United States, and wholesale the cocaine in smaller lots within the United States. The big Colombian syndicates do not form a cartel in the sense of being able to maintain prices (cocaine wholesale prices in the United States dropped from $55,000 per kilo in 1980 to $15,000 in mid-1988). These syndicates probably do not control more than 70 percent of the total world trade in cocaine; competition comes from Colombia independents and from those Bolivian and Peruvian refiners who can market their product in the United States. There is bad blood between the Medellín and Cali groups, stemming from Medellín's attempts to poach on Cali's sales territory in New York City. Yet, there is considerable business collaboration within each group: Traffickers cooperate on insuring cocaine shipments, engage in joint ventures, exchange loads, and jointly plan assassinations. Moreover, cocaine barons share a common political agenda that includes blocking the extradition of drug traffickers, immobilizing the criminal justice system, and selectively persecuting the Colombian left.

The 20-30 percent of the Colombian trade not controlled by syndicate is distributed among scattered small processors and refiners who often have links to Revolutionary Armed Forces of Colombia (FARC) guerrillas. In fact, the FARC may possess its own cocaine processing capability in some regions. The small producers cannot access the cocaine mafia's distribution capabilities; they rely heavily on mules (hired couriers) to smuggle cocaine into the United States. The top tier of the Colombian cocaine elite comprises approximately 100 people, many on the U.S. gov- ernment's list of "extraditables." At the apex of the trafficking pyramid are seven men: five Medellín-based capos—Jorge Ochoa Vazquez and his brothers Fabio and Juan David, Pablo Escobar Gaviria, and Jose Gonzalo Rodriguez Gacha from the town of Pacho in Cundinamarca—and two Cali drug lords, Gilberto Rodriguez Orejuela and Jose Santa Cruz Londono. Pablo Escobar, Jorge Ochoa and Gonzalo Rodriguez are reputably three of the world's richest men: they made *Forbes* Magazine's July 1988 list of 125 non-U.S. billionaires. By the end of the mid-1980s, the Medellín and Cali organizations together probably grossed $3 billion to $4 billion annually from international cocaine sales, primarily in the U.S. market—and 70 percent or more of that figure is profit. (Lee, 1989, pp. xiv-xvi, 7-9, 35-37)

TRIBALISM, AUTHORITARIANISM, NATIONALISM, AND ORGANIZED VIOLENCE IN THE MIDDLE EAST

The Middle East has long been a strange, mysterious part of the world to many Americans. Thrust rapidly into the modern age after World War I by the European powers, it has remained a region of contradictions: Ancient cultures underlie the trappings of modern nation-states. Foreign-built arms, the wealth of oil, strategic location, and the support of Eastern or Western superpowers have not diminished the value accumulated over many centuries of brutal political practices established as the means for conducting both domestic and foreign affairs. The politics of the Middle East is, at a minimum, a combination of three political traditions. This combination is little understood in the West, and the institutionalized violence that may arise out of the traditions is often misjudged. The three traditions are:

Tribalism: This involves associations, large or small, whose members are bound together by a spirit of solidarity, mutual loyalty, and obligations. These provide protection against all outsiders and a source of justice against those who violate the rights of the "tribe" or its members. Punishment for violations is also applied by individuals against outside violators. Whether by the "tribe" or by the individual, family, or friends, the punishments are severe, sometimes massive, and public as a warning to others.

Authoritarianism: This is expressed in the concentration of power in a single ruler or elite not bound by any constitutional framework. Two types of authoritarianism prevail: gentle and brutal. But historically even gentle authoritarianism was backed by the "sword" of the ruler. The gentle form prevails in today's Jordan, Morocco, Saudi Arabia, the Gulf Sheikdoms, Egypt, and Tunisia. These are countries that are homogeneous or where the rulers have won a high degree of consent from their people. In those Arab countries which are highly fragmented and where the modern rulers have not been able to achieve much legitimacy, such as Syria, Iraq, Lebanon, and North and South Yemen, brutal authoritarianism remains the practice.

The Modern Nation-State: This was a new concept imposed on the region by European powers during the breakup of the Ottoman Empire after World War I. Prior to this period political identifies in the region tended to be drawn along the lines of religious affiliation or local kin groups, while empires and their rulers tended to be seen as distant, often alien, entities. With the drawing up of the new nations, like modern Syria, Lebanon, Iraq, and so forth, the European powers imposed the institutions of liberal democracies such as parliaments, constitutions, national anthems, and political parties. These institutions have since that time been taking root and a kind of nationalism is beginning to find expression, but not on the model of the liberal Western democracies. Massive violence still reigns as a method used by brutal authoritarian national leaders in the region to insure the security of their own emerging nation-states against all dangers, foreign and domestic.

These three traditions do much to account for the contemporary massacres of diverse civilian populations in the region, sometimes by the leaders of their own nation-states. The traditions also do much to explain the hostility and violence toward the United States, especially since 1982 when that country threw its weight behind one coalition in the Middle East: Israel, Egypt, and Saudi Arabia, and against another: Syria, Libya, and Iran. For the latter nations, kidnapping, holding hostages, and suicide bombings are not necessarily acts of religious fanaticism, but may well be defined by leaders as calculated acts of diplomacy and defense. From such perspective, such violence may be seen as expressions of national policy without the risks of open conventional warfare when confronting nations of vastly superior military power.[1]

*   *   *

The existing literature will probably prove inadequate for providing an understanding of the various foreign settings in which different criminal organizations emerge, thrive, and act. Based on experience, existing materials will probably prove to be scarce with respect to given geographic areas or regions. Other materials will present insufficient details. And still others will be outdated. Problems of validity and reliability will also arise. For these and other reasons, additional materials from various informants regarding such environmental settings will almost certainly be required. But in the end, original area research by scholars themselves will almost certainly be necessary in many parts of the world significant for understanding multinational criminal organizations and their behavior. Obviously, language skills and foreign area studies will be essential training for those doing such research.

NOTE

1. Adapted from Friedman (1989).

References

Adler, F., Mueller, G. O. W., & Laufer, W. S. (1991). *Criminology*. New York: McGraw-Hill.

Adler, P. A. (1985). *Wheeling and dealing: An ethnography of an upper-level drug dealing and smuggling community*. New York: Columbia University Press.

Adler, P. A., & Adler, P. (1983). Shifts and oscillations in deviant careers: The case of upper-level drug dealers and smugglers. *Social Problems, 31*(2), 195-207.

Allen, T. B., & Polmar, N. (1988). *Merchants of treason*. New York: Doubleday Dell.

Amir, M. (1987). Combatting terrorism. In R. H. Ward & H. E. Smith (Eds.), *International terrorism: The domestic response*. Chicago: University of Illinois at Chicago, Office of International Criminal Justice.

Andrew, M. C. (1986). *Her Majesty's secret service: The making of the British intelligence community*. New York: Viking.

Annals of the American Academy of Political and Social Science, The. (1982, September).

Anslinger, H. J., & Tompkins, W. F. (1953). *The traffic in narcotics*. New York: Funk & Wagnalls.

Bagley, B. M. (1988). Drug trafficking in the Americas. *Journal of Interamerican Studies and World Affairs, 30*(2 & 3), iii.

Barlow, H. D. (1990). *Introduction to criminology: Readings in criminology* (5th ed.). Glenview, IL: Scott, Foresman/Little, Brown.

Bassiouni, M. C. (1981). Terrorism, law enforcement, and the mass media: Perspectives, problems, proposals. *Journal of Criminal Law and Criminology, 72*(1), 1-51.

Becker, H. S. (1963). *Outsiders: Studies in the sociology of deviance*. New York: Free Press.

Becker, H. S. (Ed.) (1964). *The other side: Perspectives on deviance*. New York: Free Press.

Beeching, J. (1975). *The Chinese opium wars*. New York: Harcourt Brace Jovanovich.

Blechman, B. M., & Kaplan, S. S. (1978). *Force without war: U.S. armed forces as a political instrument*. Washington, DC: Brookings Institute.

Blumer, H. (1969). *Symbolic interactionism: Perspective and method*. Englewood Cliffs, NJ: Prentice-Hall.

Bossard, A. (1990). *Transnational crime and criminal law*. Chicago: University of Illinois at Chicago, Office of International Criminal Justice.

Boyle, K., Hadden, T., & Hillyard, P. (1978). The facts on internment in Northern Ireland. In R. D. Crelinsten, D. Laberge-Altmejd, & D. Szabo, *Terrorism and criminal justice: An international perspective*. Lexington, MA: Lexington Books.

Bradlee, B. (1988). *Guts and glory: The rise and fall of Oliver North*. New York: Donald I. Fine.

Bremer, L. P. (1988). Address before the Carnegie Endowment for International Peace, April 21, 1988. *Terrorism: An International Journal, 11*(5), 345-347.

Brooke, J. (1990a, March 12). A portrait of the writer as the rising political star. *New York Times*, p. A4.

Brooke, J. (1990b, March 21). Angola sees gain in a free Namibia. *New York Times*, p. A12.

Brooke, J. (1990c, April 22). U.S. will arm Peru to fight leftists in new drug push. *New York Times*, p. 1.

Buckwalter, J. R. (Ed.). (1989). *International terrorism: The decade ahead*. Chicago: University of Illinois at Chicago, Office of International Criminal Justice.

Burke, M. (1991). Bolivia: The politics of cocaine. *Current History: A World Affairs Journal, 90*(553).

Burns, J. F. (1990, February 4). Afghans: Now they blame America. *The New York Times Magazine*, p. 20 ff.

Chambliss, W. J. (1989). State-organized crime. *Criminology, 27*(2), 183-208.

Chesneaux, J., Bastid, M., & Bergere, M. (1976). *China: From the opium wars to the 1911 revolution*. New York: Pantheon.

Chomsky, N. (1988). *The culture of terrorism*. Boston: South End Press.

Clinard, M. B., & Yeager, P. C. (1980). *Corporate crime*. New York: Free Press.

Cockburn, L. (1987). *Out of control: The story of the Reagan administration's secret war in Nicaragua, the illegal arms pipeline, and the Contra drug connection*. New York: Atlantic Monthly Press.

Cohen, A. K. (1977). The concept of criminal organisation. *The British Journal of Criminology, 17*(2), 97-111.

Constantinides, G. C. (1983). *Intelligence and espionage: An analytical bibliography*. Boulder, CO: Westview.

Corson, W. R., & Crowley, R. T. (1985). *The new KGB: Engine of Soviet power*. New York: William Morrow.

Coser, L. A. (1956). *The functions of social conflict*. New York: Free Press.

Craig, R. B. (1987). Illicit drug traffic: Implications for South American source countries. *Journal of Interamerican Studies and World Affairs, 29*(2), 1-34.

Crelinsten, R. D., Laberge-Altmejd, D., & Szabo, D. (1978). *Terrorism and criminal justice: An international perspective*. Lexington, MA: Lexington Books.

Crenwshaw, S. (1987). Countering terrorism: The British model. In R. H. Ward & H. E. Smith (Eds.), *International terrorism: The domestic response*. Chicago: University of Illinois at Chicago, Office of International Criminal Justice.

Cressey, D. R. (1972). *Criminal organization: Its elementary forms*. New York: Harper & Row.

Crossette, B. (1990, January 23). Indian government lodges first charges in weapons scandal. *New York Times*, p. A17.

Cushman, J. H. (1988, May 12). U.S. study sees China as a top arms dealer. *New York Times*, p. A18.

Dinges, J. (1990). *Our man in Panama*. New York: Random House.

Douglas, J. D., & Wakster, F. C. (1982). *The sociology of deviance: An introduction.* Boston: Little, Brown.

Duke, J. T. (1976). *Conflict and power in social life.* Provo, UT: Brigham Young University Press.

Elliott, J. D., & Gibson, L. K. (Eds.). (1978). *Contemporary terrorism: Selected readings.* Gaithersburg, MD: International Association of Chiefs of Police.

Engelberg, S., & Gerth, J. (1990, January 6). U.S. worry: What damage can Noriega do? *New York Times,* p. 1.

Fay, P. W. (1975). *The opium war: 1840-1842.* Chapel Hill: University of North Carolina Press.

Friedman, T. L. (1989). *From Beirut to Jerusalem.* New York: Farrar Straus Giroux.

Fussell, P. (1989). *Wartime: Understanding and behavior in the second world war.* New York: Oxford University Press.

Gerth, J., & Brinkley, J. (1985, September 25). Gun smuggling on the increase, U.S. aides say. *New York Times,* p. A2.

Gibbons, D. C. (1987). *Society, crime and criminal behavior* (5th ed.). Englewood Cliffs, NJ: Prentice-Hall.

Goldstein, P. J. (1982). Drugs and violent behavior. Paper presented at the Annual Meeting of the Academy of Criminal Justice Sciences, Louisville, KY.

Gross, F. (1969). Political violence and terror in nineteenth and twentieth century Russia and Eastern Europe. In *Assassination and Political Violence, Vol. 8, A Report to the National Commission on the Causes and Prevention of Violence.* Washington, DC: Government Printing Office.

Gugliotta, G., & Leen, J. (1990). *Kings of cocaine.* New York: Harper Paperbacks.

Gutman, R. (1988). *Banana diplomacy: The making of American policy in Nicaragua, 1981-1987.* New York: Simon & Schuster.

Heffernan, R., Martin, J. M., & Romano, A. T. (1982). Homicides related to drug trafficking. *Federal Probation: A Journal of Correctional Philosophy and Practice, XXXXVI(3),* 3-7.

Herman, E., & O'Sullivan, G. (1989). *The "terrorism" industry: The experts and institutions that shape our view of terror.* New York: Pantheon.

Hoffman, D. (1991, June 1). Angolans sign pact, 16 years of war end. *Boston Globe,* p. 1.

Holland, J. (1987). *The American connection: U.S. guns, money and influence in Northern Ireland.* New York: Viking.

Ianni, F. A. J., & Reuss-Ianni, E. (1972). *A family business: Kinship and social control in organized crime.* New York: Russell Sage Foundation.

Ibrahim, Y. M. (1990, January 30). Trial of accused mastermind in bombings begins in Paris. *New York Times,* p. A2.

Inciardi, J. A. (1975). *Careers in Crime.* Chicago: Rand McNally.

Inciardi, J. A. (1984). *The war on drugs: Heroin, cocaine, crime, and public policy.* Palo Alto, CA: Mayfield.

Inouye, D. K., & Hamilton, L. H. (1988). *Report of the congressional committees investigating the Iran-Contra affair.* New York: Random House.

Journal of Interamerican Studies & World Affairs. (1988). *30*(2 & 3).

Katz, J. (1977). Cover-up and collective integrity: On the natural antagonisms of authority internal and external to organizations. *Social Problems, 25*(1), 3-17.

Kelly, R. T. (Ed.). (1986). *Organized crime: A global perspective.* Totowa, NJ: Rowman & Littlefield.

Kempe, F. (1990). *Divorcing the dictator: America's bungled affair with Noriega*. New York: G. P. Putnam.

Kittrie, N. N., & Wedlock, E. D. (Eds.). (1986). *The tree of liberty: A documentary history of rebellion and political crime in America*. Baltimore: Johns Hopkins University Press.

Klare, M. T. (1988). Secret operatives, clandestine trades: The thriving black market for weapons. *Bulletin of Atomic Scientists, 44*(3), 16-24.

Klare, M. T., & Kornbluh, P. (Eds.). (1988). *Low-intensity warfare: Counterinsurgency, proinsurgency, and anti-terrorism in the eighties*. New York: Pantheon.

Klockars, C. B. (1974). *The professional fence*. New York: Free Press.

Knightley, P. (1986). *The second oldest profession: Spies and spying in the twentieth century*. New York: Penguin.

Krauss, C. (1991, August 7). U.S. military team to advise Peru in war against drugs and rebels. *New York Times*, p. A1.

Kriesberg, L. (1973). *The sociology of social conflicts*. Englewood Cliffs, NJ: Prentice-Hall.

Kupperman, R. H. (1985). Terrorism and public policy: Domestic impacts, international threats. In L. A. Curtis (Ed.), *American violence and public policy*. New Haven: Yale University Press.

Kurjian, S. (1991, May 19). U.S. debates tinkering, tailoring at the CIA. *Boston Sunday Globe*, p. 1.

Kwitny, J. (187). *The crimes of patriots: A true tale of dope, dirty money, and the CIA*. New York: Norton.

Lamour, C., & Lamberti, M. R. (1974). *The international connection*. New York: Pantheon.

Lee, R. W. III (1989). *The white labyrinth: Cocaine and political power*. New Brunswick, NJ: Transaction Books.

Lewis, P. (1990, February 21). Drugs pit Baker vs. third world at U.N. *New York Times*, p. A3.

Liebow, E. (1967). *Tally's corner: A study of Negro street-corner men*. Boston: Little, Brown.

Lifton, R. J. (1986). *The Nazi doctors: Medical killing and the psychology of genocide*. New York: Basic Books.

Long, D. E. (1990). *The anatomy of terrorism*. New York: Free Press.

Lopez-Rey, M. (1974). United Nations social defense policy and the problem of crime. In R. Hook (Ed.), *Crime, criminology and public policy*. New York: Free Press.

Lupsha, P. A. (1981). Drug trafficking: Mexico and Colombia in comparative perspective. *Journal of International Affairs, 35*(1), 95-115.

Lupsha, P. A. (1988). The role of drugs and drug trafficking in the invisible wars. In D. Rowe (Ed.), *International drug trafficking*. Chicago: University of Illinois at Chicago, Office of International Criminal Justice.

Maas, P. (1986). *Manhunt*. New York: Random House.

Macartney, J. (1988). Intelligence: A consumer's guide. *International Journal of Intelligence and Counter-intelligence, 2*(4), 1-30.

Mack, J. A. (1975). *The crime industry*. Lexington, MA: Lexington Books.

Marquis, C. (1990, January 10). Panamanians buy up guns fearing chaos after pullout. *Miami Herald*, p. 1.

Massing, M. (1990, March 4). In the cocaine war . . . the jungle is winning. *The New York Times Magazine*, p. 26 ff.

McCoy, A. W. (1980). *Drug traffic: Narcotics and organized crime in Australia.* Sydney: Norton.

McCoy, A. W. (1986). Organized crime in Australia: An urban history. In R. J. Kelly (Ed.), *Organized crime: A global perspective.* Totowa, NJ: Rowman & Littlefield.

McCoy, A. W., Read, C. B., & Adams, L. P. (1972). *The politics of heroin in southeast Asia.* New York: Harper & Row.

McFadden, R. D. (1984, April 16). 10 in Brooklyn are found slain inside a house. *New York Times,* p. 1.

Meier, R. F. (1989). *Crime and society.* Boston: Allyn & Bacon.

Miller, R. (1988). The literature of terrorism. *Terrorism: An International Journal, 11*(1).

Mills, J. (1986). *The underground empire: Where crime and governments embrace.* New York: Doubleday.

Moore, M. H. (1986). *Organized crime as a business enterprise.* Unpublished manuscript. Cambridge, MA: Harvard University, J. F. Kennedy School of Government.

Moore, M. H. (1989). *Supply reduction and drug law enforcement.* Unpublished manuscript. Cambridge, MA: Harvard University, J. F. Kennedy School of Government.

Morales, E. (1986). Coca and cocaine economy and social change in the Andes of Peru. *Economic Development and Cultural Change, 35*(1), 143-161.

Moscow reports the capture of a longtime American spy. (1990, January 15). *New York Times,* p. 1.

Moynihan, D. P. (1990). *On the law of nations.* Cambridge, MA: Harvard University Press.

Musto, D. F. (1987). *The American disease: Origins of narcotic control.* New York: Oxford University Press.

Nash, N. (1991, August 11). The challenge in Peru: Drugs and disarray. *New York Times,* sec. 4, p. 3.

Penn, S. (1990, March 22). Asian connection: Chinese gangsters fill a narcotics gap left by U.S. drive on Mafia. *Wall Street Journal,* p. 1.

Phillips, K. (1990). *The politics of rich and poor.* New York: Random House.

Pierre, A. J. (1982). *The global politics of arms sales.* Princeton, NJ: Princeton University Press.

Pincher, C. (1987). *Traitors: The anatomy of treason.* New York: St. Martin's Press.

Pipes, D. (1988). Why Assad's terror works and Qadhafi's does not. *Terrorism: An International Journal, 11*(5), 364-369.

Polsky, N. (1967). *Hustlers, beats and others.* Chicago: Aldine.

Posner, G. L. (1988). *Warlords of crime: Chinese secret societies—the new Mafia.* New York: McGraw-Hill.

Prange, G. W., Goldstein, D. M., and Dillon, K. V. (1984). *Target Tokyo: The story of the Sorge spy ring.* New York: McGraw-Hill.

Preble, E., & Casey, J. J. (1969). Taking care of business—the heroin user's life on the street. *The International Journal of the Addictions, 4*(1), 1-24.

Protzman, F. (1989, December 1). Head of top West German bank is killed in bombing by terrorists. *New York Times,* p. A1.

Radzinowicz, L. (1966). *Ideology and crime.* New York: Columbia University Press.

Ranelagh, J. (1986). *The agency: The rise and decline of the CIA.* New York: Simon & Schuster.

Raviv, D., & Melman, Y. (1990). *Every spy a prince: The complete history of Israel's intelligence community.* Boston: Houghton Mifflin.

Reid, S. T. (1988). *Crime and criminology* (5th ed.). New York: Holt, Rinehart & Winston.

Rice, B. (1989). *Trafficking: The boom and bust of the Air America cocaine ring*. New York: Scribner.

Rohter, L. (1990, February 2). U.S. charges in drug agent's death: New friction. *New York Times*, p. A14.

Romano, A. T. (1984). *Terrorism: An analysis of the literature*. Unpublished doctoral dissertation, Fordham University.

Rositzke, H. A. (1977). *The CIA's secret operations*. New York: Reader's Digest Press.

Rouqié, A. (1987). *The military and the state in Latin America*. Berkeley: University of California Press.

Royal Canadian Mounted Police (1988). *National Drug intelligence estimate 1986/87*. Ottawa, Ontario, Canada.

Sampson, A. (1977). *The arms bazaar: From Lebanon to Lockheed*. New York: Viking.

Schafer, S. (1974). *The political criminal*. New York: Free Press.

Sciolino, E. (1987, January 13). U.S. report links drugs, arms traffic and terror. *New York Times*, p. B7.

Sciolino, E. (1990, March 2). World drug crop up sharply in 1989 despite U.S. effort. *New York Times*, p. 1.

Sellin, T. (1938). *Culture conflict and crime*. New York: Social Science Research Council.

Shenon, P. (1984, April 17). Drug link is seen in slayings of 10. *New York Times*, p. 1.

Siegel, L. J. (1986). *Criminology* (2nd ed.). St. Paul: West.

Smith, H. E. (Ed.). (1989). *Transnational crime: Investigative responses*. Chicago: University of Illinois at Chicago, Office of International Criminal Justice.

Steinitz, M. S. (1985). Insurgents, terrorists and the drug trade. *The Washington Quarterly, 8*(4), 141-153.

Sterling, C. (1990). *Octopus: The long reach of the international Sicilian Mafia*. New York: Norton.

Stockwell, J. (1978). *In search of enemies: A CIA story*. New York: Norton.

Sutherland, E. H. (1937). *The professional thief*. Chicago: University of Chicago Press.

Taylor, A. H. (1969). *American diplomacy and the narcotics traffic, 1900-1939*. Durham, NC: Duke University Press.

Thayer, G. (1969). *The war business: The international trade in armaments*. New York: Simon & Schuster.

Thrasher, F. M. (1927). *The gang: A study of 1,313 gangs in Chicago*. Chicago: University of Chicago Press.

Throw, R., Aeppel, T., Mossberg, W. S., & Sesit, M. R. (1989, December 1). European shock: Terrorist murder stuns a Germany euphoric over rapprochement. *Wall Street Journal*, p. A1.

Treaster, J. B. (1991, August 13). Cocaine is again surging out of Panama. *New York Times*, p. A1.

Treverton, G. F. (1987). *Covert action: The limits of intervention in the postwar world*. New York: Basic Books.

Turk, A. T. (1982). *Political criminality*. Beverly Hills, CA: Sage.

U.S. Attorney General's Report. (1989). *Drug trafficking: A report to the President of the United States*.

U.S. Bureau of Alcohol, Tobacco & Firearms (n.d.). *Trace study: New York City January 1981–August 1983*. Washington, DC: U.S. Treasury Department.

U.S. Bureau of Alcohol, Tobacco & Firearms. (1989, June 1). *News*. Washington, DC: U.S. Treasury Department.

U.S. Bureau of Alcohol, Tobacco & Firearms. (1989, September 1). *News*. Washington, DC: U.S. Treasury Department.

U.S. Department of Justice. (1988). *National Institute of Justice, research program plan, fiscal year 1989*. Washington, DC: Government Printing Office.

U.S. Drug Enforcement Administration. (1989). *EPIC special report*. Washington, DC: U.S. Department of Justice.

Vold, G. B., & Bernard, T. J. (1986). *Theoretical criminology* (3rd ed.). New York: Oxford University Press.

Waint, J. A. (1985). Narcotics in the Golden Triangle. *The Washington Quarterly, 8*(4), 125-140.

Wakefield, D. (1959). *Island in the city: The world of Spanish Harlem*. Boston: Houghton Mifflin.

Ward, R. H., & Smith, H. E. (Eds.). (1987). *International terrorism: The domestic response*. Chicago: University of Illinois at Chicago, Office of International Criminal Justice.

Ward, R. H., & Smith, H. E. (Eds.). (1988). *International terrorism: Operational issues*. Chicago: University of Illinois at Chicago, Office of International Criminal Justice.

Washington Quarterly, The. (1985). *8*(1).

White House, The. (1989). *National drug control strategy*. Washington, DC.

Whyte, W. F. (1955). *Street corner society* (Enlarged 2nd ed.). Chicago: University of Chicago Press.

Williams, F. P., & McShane, M. D. (1988). *Criminological theory*. Englewood Cliffs, NJ: Prentice-Hall.

Wise, D. (1988). *The spy who got away*. New York: Random House.

Woodward, B. (1991). *The commanders*. New York: Simon & Schuster.

Wright, J. (1986). *Torture in Brazil*. New York: Vintage.

Wright, P. (1987). *Spy catcher*. New York: Dell.

Author Index

Subject Index

About the Authors

John M. Martin is Professor of Sociology and former Chairman of the Department of Sociology and Anthropology at Fordham University. During its brief and stormy history, he was also Director, Graduate Program in Criminal Justice at Fordham. He has published three books on delinquency theory and methods, and numerous essays and articles on such topics as the politics of delinquency, drug-abuse treatment, bank robbery, drug-related homicide, and international crime.

Anne T. Romano is Adjunct Assistant Professor, Department of Sociology, Nassau Community College; Department of Criminal Justice and Security Administration, Long Island University—C. W. Post College; St. John's University; and the Department of Behavioral Sciences at Kingsborough College in New York. She is also the author of several books on human relations for 911 operators and police personnel, and has published articles on spouse- and child-abuse patterns, terrorism, drug-related homicide, and drug-trafficking.